The Young Readers' Guide to Understanding the Bible

Aaron Homer

iUniverse, Inc.
New York   Bloomington

The Young Readers' Guide to Understanding the Bible

iUniverse books may be ordered through booksellers or by contacting:

iUniverse
1663 Liberty Drive
Bloomington, IN 47403
www.iuniverse.com
1-800-Authors (1-800-288-4677)

Because of the dynamic nature of the Internet, any Web addresses or links contained in this book may have changed since publication and may no longer be valid.

ISBN: 978-1-4401-9855-7 (sc)
ISBN: 978-1-4401-9856-4 (ebk)

Printed in the United States of America

iUniverse rev. date: 12/23/2009

Contents

This is where you will learn about how the Bible came to be, how Bible scholars approach studying the Bible, and other basic information about the Bible.

In this chapter you'll learn about the very earliest history recorded in the Bible, all of which we learn about in the book of Genesis.

This chapter introduces you to a major event in Old Testament history called the Exodus. This story is told mostly over two books: Exodus and Numbers.

This chapter will teach you about the laws that God expected His people to follow in Old Testament times. This may sound boring, but it really isn't! Knowing about Old Testament law will be really important in helping you understand Jesus' ministry.

In this chapter you'll learn about several hundred years of history of God's people from the time they first arrived in the home God chose for them, until about 400 years before Jesus was born.

This chapter will teach you about the poetry and prophecy of the Old Testament, and how some of it teaches about Jesus.

This chapter is about what happened in the 400 years between the time the last words of the Old Testament were written until when Jesus was born.

This chapter is about the books Bible scholars call the Gospels (Matthew, Mark, Luke and John). Here we learn about Jesus, His ministry, and His death and resurrection.

This chapter is about the book in the Bible (Acts) that teaches us about the early history of the Christian Church.

This chapter is about a major part of the New Testament: the Epistles (letters) that were written to early Christians. And don't worry: you'll find out what the terms "Pauline Epistles" and "General Epistles" mean!

In this chapter you'll learn about the most misunderstood and misused book in the entire Bible: Revelation.

NOTE TO PARENTS

Most of the Bible education that our children receive in the church today is in the form of stories, often taken out of context and with little to no explanation as to their cultural or historical background. Our kids may learn about the king of Babylon throwing Daniel in the lion's den, but who is Daniel, and why was he in Babylon? They may learn about Paul's shipwreck, but who is Paul, and why was he on a ship? They may learn about Jesus healing a blind man by spitting on the ground to make clay that healed the blind man's eyes, but they don't learn that Jesus spitting on the ground upset the leaders of His day so much that they didn't care about the blind man being healed.

No single resource puts all of those Bible stories into context, in a way that children can understand. Daniel in the lion's den is a good story that teaches a good moral, and most Christian children are familiar with it. Jesus healing the blind man is also a good story with a good moral that most Christian children have heard, as is the story of Paul's shipwreck. But how many Christian children know that Daniel's (and the Israelites') captivity in Babylon shaped the culture in which Jesus spitting on the ground was so upsetting to the leaders? Or that the same leaders who got upset at Jesus spitting on the ground got so upset with Paul that he wound up on a ship that got shipwrecked?

That is the purpose of this book: to provide a narrative of Bible history, from beginning to end, and hitting on the high and low points, so that all those Bible stories will have a context. Additionally, this book explains the significance of the non-historical books of the Bible; that is, the significance of the books of poetry, the books of prophecy, and the epistles. If the Bible stories, Bible verses, and memory work that your kids have learned through the teaching ministry of your church are the bricks, this book provides the mortar.

Although I've tried to make the language in this book as understandable as possible, even to new readers, the ideal age group for this book is kids at a fourth-grade or higher reading level. Additionally, this book will touch upon some concepts (such as adultery) that are best discussed with a parent or youth leader. I recommend that parents and/or youth leaders read this book *with* their children, and be available to answer any questions that young readers may have.

The child who reads this book will, when he or she hears a lesson about Daniel in the lion's Den, know who Daniel was and why he and his people were in captivity. The child who reads this book will, when sitting in church and hearing the minister mention Paul's letter to the Corinthians, know who Paul was, who the Corinthians were, and why Paul wrote a letter to them. This book will not teach a child everything that there is to know about the Bible, but it's comprehensive enough to be a starting point for your child's journey of faith.

NOTE: By necessity, this book will touch upon some matters about which Christians debate with each other, including (but not limited to): the KJV-only controversy, the authorship of Hebrews, the tongues-speaking controversy, and the interpretation of prophecy. In these cases, I defer to the prevailing scholarship among evangelical Christian scholars about these controversies, but remind the reader that there is debate about these things, and that such debates are not the purpose of this book.

INTRODUCTION

Congratulations on picking up this book! The fact that you have it in your hands means that you, or a parent, a loved one, or one of your youth leaders has decided that you are ready to learn more about the Bible. Good for you! You are about to begin a journey that will last the rest of your life.

Many kids are intimidated by the Bible – after all, the Bible is long, contains lots of big words, has lots of long names of people and places, and talks about things that are difficult to understand. That's what this book is for – to help you make sense of the Bible. But let me warn you now: this book is a long book, and you may feel dizzy with too much information if you try to read it all at once. My advice is to take this book in small doses. Read only a few pages at a time, so your brain will have time to take it all in, and so you don't get bogged down in lots of small details.

You will probably never fully understand every word of the Bible, and that's OK. The Bible has been studied for centuries, and thousands of Bible scholars have devoted their entire lives to studying it, and even today the meaning of certain parts of the Bible are debated by Bible scholars all over the world. But that's OK, too, because the important parts of the Bible *are* clear and *are* easy to understand. And the most important part of the Bible is this:

> *For God loved the world so much that He gave His one and only Son; that whoever believes in Him will not perish, but have eternal life. John 3:16 New Living Translation*

The clear message of the Bible is this: God sent His son, Jesus, to die for the sins of the world, and He wants to have a relationship with you. Everything else in the Bible explains the how's and the why's. But for now, the most important thing you can take from the Bible is this: God loves you, God sent His son Jesus to die for you, and God wants to have a relationship with you.

If you do not already have a relationship with God, I encourage you to talk to a parent, your children's minister, your pastor, or a youth leader to see if you are ready to make that commitment.

Finally, let me encourage you to make the most of every opportunity you have to learn about God and the Bible. God has placed youth leaders, pastors, and other teachers into your life so that you can learn about Him. Make the most of it! Commit, right now, to going to church and Sunday School every Sunday; to going to every camp, Vacation Bible School, kids' night out… to every activity that your church offers you; and to doing your best to pay attention to your teachers and leaders and to learning everything that God wants to teach you through them.

CHAPTER 1

THE BASICS

The Bible is not one book, but a collection of sixty six books. It is divided into two parts: the Old Testament and the New Testament. The Old Testament teaches us about how God worked in history to set the stage for the arrival of Jesus, the savior. The New Testament tells the story of Jesus' ministry on Earth, tells the history of the early Christian church, and provides a collection of letters that were written by early Christian leaders to the church.

WHAT THE BIBLE IS NOT, AND WHAT THE BIBLE IS

Before we move on, it's a good idea to talk about some misconceptions (wrong ideas) that people may have about the Bible.

The Bible is **not** a "magic" book. It does not contain spells that you can use to bring about things that you want. Carrying one in your pocket will not necessarily protect you from harm. You cannot simply open it up to a random page, and pick out a random verse, and find something meaningful.

To understand how to properly read the Bible, let's compare it to another great work of literature, Mark Twain's book *The Adventures of Tom Sawyer*. You may have been assigned to read *Tom Sawyer* in school; if you haven't yet, believe me, you will someday! *Tom Sawyer* was written in 1876, and it's about the adventures of a naughty young boy growing up in rural Missouri before the Civil War.

Imagine if you opened up to a random page in *Tom Sawyer* and read a few sentences. If you haven't read the book before, those few sentences you read won't make any sense. Say that you read a passage where Tom is speaking. Since boys and girls in rural Missouri in the 1800's spoke differently than you do now, you may not understand some of what Tom is saying. Say you read a passage where Tom is in a cave; that's great, but why is Tom in a cave? Say you read a passage where Tom sneaks in on a funeral; funerals are sad, and you may feel sad for the characters at the funeral, but whose funeral is it, and why is Tom sneaking into it?

If all you get of *Tom Sawyer* is a few sentences here and there, without knowing the whole story and without knowing any *context* (don't worry: I'll tell you what "context" means in a little bit!), you're not going to understand it. Also, if you don't understand what life was like in rural Missouri in the 1800's, there's a lot of it that you won't understand. If you don't have a dictionary and don't have a way of understanding some of the things the characters say, there's a lot of it you won't understand.

It's the same with the Bible! Most Christian kids learn the Bible by hearing stories here and there (in Sunday School, for example), but you don't learn the *context* of those stories. Your minister may read a verse or a passage in his sermon, but you might not know the *context* of those passages. So what does this word "context" mean that I keep using? It's a fancy way of saying "the whole thing." If you've read *Tom Sawyer* from beginning to end, then when someone talks about Tom being in a cave, you'll remember the story and why Tom was in the cave, and it will make more sense to you. With the Bible, you may hear a Sunday School lesson about Paul being shipwrecked; if you know the context, you'll know who Paul was, and how he wound up being shipwrecked.

That's what this book is all about: giving you the *context* of just about everything that's written in the Bible, from beginning to end. Don't worry, I leave out quite a bit! But the things I leave in are the things that you're likely to learn about at church, or that you're likely to hear your minister talk about when he preaches. When you've finished this book, you'll know all of the major things that happened in the Bible, from Page 1 in Genesis through the final page of Revelation.

There are other things you need to know about to understand the Bible as well. Let's go back to *Tom Sawyer*. To fully understand *Tom Sawyer*, you would do well to understand what rural Missouri is like, what life in the 1850's was like, and how people spoke in the 1850's. It's the same with the Bible; to fully understand the Bible, you would do well to understand the *geography* (places on maps) of Bible lands, the *cultures* (how people acted and how people treated each other) of Bible times, and the language used in the Bible.

Most of the Bible is written in what is called *narrative* (a fancy word that means a summary of what happened). Some of it is written to read like a poem. The Bible contains lots of figures of speech. Some passages in the Bible contain the words of someone pouring out their anger and hate, describing in gruesome detail the things they'd like to do to their enemies. Several hundred pages of the Bible are precise instructions on how God expected His people to live their lives.

In light of the information I gave you in the paragraphs above this one, you may think that you're in over your head. Don't worry! Even though, as I said, you'll probably never understand every word of the Bible, if you read this book, you'll understand enough to start you on your life-long journey of learning about what God has to say. In fact, if you read all of this book, cover to cover, you'll actually know more about the Bible than I first did when I enrolled in Bible College when I was 22 years old!

HOW DID THE BIBLE COME TO BE?

The Bible did not suddenly fall out of the sky and into the laps of church leaders. Actually, the Bible was written over the course of several thousand years, by several different people, and in several different languages. One interesting thing to note about the Bible is that, though several different men put pen to paper to create the Bible, every last word on every page came directly from God. This is why we say the Bible is *inspired* by God – because God directed the writers as they put their words on the pages.

Bible scholars debate with each other over exactly how God inspired the writers of the Bible. Some believe that God's spirit actually pushed the pens in the writers' hands; others believe that God put the words directly into the authors' minds; still others believe that God worked in different ways. However God inspired the authors, what is important to know is that God used these men to deliver the words that He wants us to know.

The original pages on which the authors of the Bible wrote their words (Bible scholars call these pages *autographs*) are long lost to history. However, they were copied, by hand, time and time again over the course of centuries. Remember, this was in the days before photocopiers or even the printing press, which means that one copy could take someone years to make! These handwritten copies (called *texts* by Bible scholars) were copied again and again, generation after generation, until the invention of the printing press, which made hand-copying obsolete.

It was these ancient, hand-copied texts that were compiled into the book we now know as the Bible. The invention of the printing press in 1439 meant that Bibles could be printed relatively quickly, and in mass quantities, meaning that Bibles no longer needed to be hand-copied. NOTE: There is a lot more to the story than what I've given in these few paragraphs. For a much more thorough history of how the Bible came about, read *How We Got the Bible*, by Neil R. Lightfoot.

BOOK, CHAPTER AND VERSE

As I said earlier, the Bible is divided into two halves, the Old Testament and the New Testament, and it is divided even further into sixty six books. The Old Testament has thirty nine books, and the New Testament has twenty seven. Each book in the Bible (with a couple of exceptions) is further broken down into chapters, and even further into verses. (The Bible has over 66,000 verses!).

When the writers of the Bible wrote their original words, they did not divide them up into chapters and verses. Those were a later addition. The Old Testament was broken down into verses over the course of several centuries, but the current pattern of verses in the Old Testament can most certainly be credited to a Jewish Rabbi (teacher) by the name of Isaac Nathan. The New Testament, on the other hand, was broken down into chapters and verses by a 13th-century Christian named Stephen Langton.

When you read about a Bible passage on paper, you will almost always read the name of the book, followed by the chapter of the book, then a colon (:), then the verse. For example: Proverbs 16:3. In this case, this refers to the book of Proverbs, chapter 16, verse three. When saying the name of a Bible passage, you don't mention the colon. So Proverbs 16:3 would be said as "Proverbs sixteen three," or "Proverbs sixteen, verse 3."

There are some books in the Bible where two (or in one case, three) books share the same name. For example, there are two books entitled "Kings." In this case, the first book of Kings will have the number 1 before it, and the second book will have the number 2 before it. On paper it would look like this: 1 Kings or 2 Kings, and you would say it as "First Kings" or "Second Kings."

There are also some books in the Bible that are so short that there's no need to break them up into chapters. For example, the book of Philemon (Fye-LEE-mun) has no chapters. To find a verse in a book with no chapters, you just say the name of the book and then the name of the verse. So the first verse of Philemon is simply Philemon 1, and you would say it as "Philemon one."

To practice learning how Bible verses are identified, try the following exercises:

1. How would you tell someone to find the fourth verse of the fifth chapter of the book of Exodus?

2. How would you tell someone to find the seventh verse of the second chapter of the second book of Timothy?

    _____

3. How would you tell someone to find the ninth verse of the book of Philemon?

    _____

DIVIDING UP THE BOOKS

As I said a few pages ago, the Bible is divided into two parts; the Old Testament and the New Testament. Each testament can be divided into smaller sections. Knowing what these sections are, and the names of the books within them, will help you as you learn what they mean in later chapters. *In the next few pages you're going to see some big names that you may not know how to pronounce. For now, don't worry about how to pronounce them. We'll work on that later in the book.

THE OLD TESTAMENT

Take a look at your left hand. You should see a thumb and then four fingers. With your right hand, point to your thumb and say the word "Five." Next, point to your index finger (the finger you point with) and say the word "Twelve." Next, point to your middle finger and say the world "Five." Point to the next finger and say "Five." Finally, point to your pinky and say "Twelve." Go through each finger again, saying that finger's number each time. "5 – 12 – 5 – 5 – 12."

The first five books of the Old Testament are called the five books of the **Law** (don't worry, you'll learn what that means later in this book). The five books of the **Law** are Genesis, Exodus, Leviticus, Numbers, and Deuteronomy.

The next section of the Old Testament is the twelve books of **History**. They are Joshua, Judges, Ruth, 1 Samuel, 2 Samuel, 1 Kings, 2 Kings, 1 Chronicles, 2 Chronicles, Ezra, Nehemiah, and Esther.

The next section of the Old Testament is the five books of **Poetry**. They are Job, Psalms, Proverbs, Ecclesiastes, and Song of Songs (or in some Bibles Song of Solomon).

The next section of the Old Testament is the five books of the **Major Prophets**. They are: Isaiah, Jeremiah, Lamentation, Ezekiel, and Daniel.

The last section of the Old Testament is the twelve books of the **Minor Prophets**. They are Hosea, Joel, Amos, Obadiah, Jonah, Michal, Nahum, Habakkuk, Zephaniah, Haggai, Zechariah, and Malachi.

If you *really* want to impress your friends, parents, or youth leaders, memorize the 39 books of Old Testament in order. Use the 5 – 12 – 5 – 5 – 12 pattern to help you; memorize the names of the books in each section, then say them all together, each section in order. On the next page is a list of the Old Testament books, in order. Good luck!

5 Law	Genesis (JEN-uh-sis) Exodus (EX-uh-dus) Leviticus (luh-VIT-uh-cus) Numbers Deuteronomy (doo-ter-OHN-uh-mee)
12 History	Joshua Judges Ruth 1 Samuel 2 Samuel 1 Kings 2 Kings 1 Chronicles (KRON-ih-culs) 2 Chronicles Ezra Nehemiah (nee-uh-MYE-uh) Esther
5 Poetry	Job (JOBE) Psalms (pronounced without the P) Proverbs Ecclesiastes (uh-cleez-ee-ASS-teez) Song of Songs
5 Major Prophets	Isaiah (eye-ZAY-uh) Jeremiah (jair-uh-MYE-uh) Lamentations (lam-en-TAY-shuns) Ezekiel (ee-ZEE-kee-uhl) Daniel
12 Minor Prophets	Hosea (hose-AY-uh) Joel Amos (AY-mus) Obadiah (oh-buh-DIE-uh) Jonah (JOE-nuh) Micah (MY-cuh) Nahum (NAY-hum) Habakkuk (huh-BACK-uhk) Zephaniah (zef-uh-NYE-uh) Haggai (HAG-guy) Zechariah (zeck-uh-RYE-uh) Malachi (MAL-uh-kye)

The New Testament

Remember how we started learning about the Old Testament by looking at your left hand? Now, let's do the second half of the Bible, the New Testament. Take a look at your right hand. You should see your pinky, three more fingers, then your thumb. Point to your pinky and say "Four." Next, point to your next finger and say "One." Point to your middle finger and say "Thirteen." Point to your next finger and say "Eight." Finally, point to your thumb and say "One." Go through each finger again, saying each finger's number: "4 – 1 – 13 – 8 – 1."

The first four books of the New Testament are called the **Gospels**. Don't worry, we'll learn what that word means later in the book. The four books of the Gospels are Matthew, Mark, Luke and John.

The next section of the New Testament is only one book. It's the **History** section, and it contains the New Testament's one history book, the book of Acts.

The next section of the New Testament is a big one: it's the thirteen books that are referred to as the **Pauline Epistles** (paul-EEN eh-PIST-uls). Don't worry, you'll find out what the phrase "Pauline Epistles" means later in this book! The Pauline Epistles are Romans, 1 Corinthians, 2 Corinthians, Galatians, Ephesians, Philippians, Colossians, 1 Thessalonians, 2 Thessalonians, 1 Timothy, 2 Timothy, Titus, and Philemon.

The next section of the New Testament is the eight books known as the **General Epistles**. Don't worry, you'll find out what the phrase "General Epistles" means later in this book! The General Epistles are Hebrews, James, 1 Peter, 2 Peter, 1 John, 2 John, 3 John and Jude.

The last section of the New Testament is the one book of **Prophecy**. The one book of Prophecy is Revelation. Note: You may hear people refer to this last book as the book of Revelations (with an s at the end); that is incorrect. There is no s at the end. Please show respect to the person who wrote it (God) and say it correctly!

If you *really* want to impress your friends, parents, or youth leaders, memorize the 27 books of New Testament in order. Use the 4 – 1 – 13 – 8 – 1 pattern to help you; memorize the names of the books in each section, then say them all together, each section in order. On the next page is a list of the New Testament books, in order. Good luck!

4 Gospel

Matthew
Mark
Luke
John

1 History

Acts

13 Pauline Epistles

Romans
1 Corinthians (core-INN-thee-ans)
2 Corinthians
Galatians (guh-LAY-shuns)
Ephesians (eh-FEE-zhuns)
Philippians (fill-IPP-ee-uhns)
Colossians (cuhl-OSS-yuns)
1 Thessalonians (thess-a-LOW-nee-uhns)
2 Thessalonians
1 Timothy
2 Timothy
Titus (TIGHT-us)
Philemon (fye-LEE-mon)

8 General Epistles

Hebrews
James
1 Peter
2 Peter
1 John
2 John
3 John
Jude

1 Prophecy

Revelation

A Matter Of Translation

Even though the Bible you read is in English, it wasn't written in English. In fact, the English language didn't even exist when the Bible was written! The Bible was actually written in three languages. Most of the Old Testament was written in a language called Hebrew, and a small part of the Old Testament was written in a language called Aramaic (air-uh-MAY-ick). The New Testament was written in a language called Greek.

Since most of the people in the world can't read Hebrew, Aramaic, or Greek (or all three), it makes sense to translate the Bible into the language that the reader speaks. In your case, you're reading an English translation, but there are also translations into Spanish, French, Chinese… just about every language in the world. In fact, one of the most important jobs that some missionaries have is translating the Bible into languages that don't yet have a translation (a missionary is a person who goes to foreign countries to teach about Jesus).

There are actually several English translations, and you have a variety to choose from when you buy a Bible. One of the first English translations, which is still very popular to this day, is called the King James Version (KJV). You may have heard someone read a passage from the KJV before; if you hear a lot of words that sound like "thee" and "thou" and "thine" and "thou art" and "thou shalt," chances are it's from the KJV. The KJV has the advantage of being very traditional and it sounds very solemn, but it's also very difficult to read, especially for young people.

Probably the most popular English translation for Christians in the United States is the New International Version (NIV). In fact, if you showed me ten kids who have read *The Young Readers' Guide to Understanding the Bible*, it's a safe bet that nine of them have an NIV translation of the Bible. The NIV has the advantage of being both popular and being easy to read.

There are other English translations of the Bible as well. Some of them are even easier to read than the NIV, and many are written especially for kids. Some other good translations are the Contemporary English Version (CEV) and the New Living Translation (NLT).

When someone is writing a book, article, Sunday School lesson, etc. and they want to quote a passage from the Bible, it's good manners to tell the reader the name of the translation you're quoting from. The author will usually say the name of the translation after he or she writes the name of the book, chapter and verse. For example, take a look at the Introduction to this book, where I quoted John 3:16. You'll notice that I wrote the words "New Living Translation" after I wrote the words "John 3:16." That's because the passage I quoted was from the New Living Translation. Telling the reader what translation you're using serves two purposes: first, it lets the reader know what translation they're reading so they don't get confused; and second, it gives credit to and shows respect to the scholars who wrote the translation.

One of the things Bible scholars love debating about is which translations are better and which translations are worse. You may even meet some people in your life who believe very strongly that the King James Version (KJV) is the only English translation that honors God, and the only one that English-speaking Christians should use. Others may argue that one translation is bad for this reason, another translation is bad for that reason, and so on. These debates are best left to Bible scholars and are not the focus of this book. The best translation for you is the one that you, your parents, and your youth leaders at church all agree on.

Now, grab a Bible, preferably in a translation that is easy for you to read. Keep it with you as read this book, because we're going to be referring to it quite often. Most likely, your parents or someone else who loves you has already given you your own copy, but if you don't have one, borrow one. Better yet, ask a parent to get you one; if they can't, ask a youth leader at your church – they'll be only too happy to give you one! Also, grab a dictionary. Bible scholars like to impress each other by using fancy words! And even though I've tried my hardest to use words you'll understand, or to explain what the fancy words mean whenever I have to use a fancy one, you still might find that I use some words you don't understand.

CHAPTER TWO

OLD TESTAMENT LAW PART 1: GENESIS

Bible scholars refer to the Old Testament's first five books as the books of The Law. That's because a major part of these five books is just that: law. God gave instructions (laws), some of them *very* specific, on how He wanted His people to live their lives, and those laws are contained in these five books. The rest of these first five books contain quite a bit of history, and that's what we're going to focus on in this chapter and the next. Most importantly, these five books, written by Moses (who will come into play in the book of Exodus), represent the foundation on which the entire religion of Judaism* (JUDE-ay-ism), and on which the whole rest of the Bible, is built. *Don't worry, we'll learn about the significance of Judaism later in this chapter.

Before we get started, here's a quick note about place names: Turn to the back of your Bible – the publisher of your Bible should have given you some maps. If not, have a parent or a teacher help you with an atlas (a book of maps) or help you get on the internet, and find a map of the Mediterranean Sea. If you really stretch your imagination, you can imagine that the Mediterranean Sea looks like a hot dog lying on its side. On the right hand side of the hot dog is the eastern shore of the Mediterranean Sea. Just about everything that happens in the Bible takes place within a few hundred miles of the eastern shore of the Mediterranean Sea.

For now, we won't worry about any specific places, since the Bible doesn't start giving us names of places that we know about for certain for quite a few chapters.

Part 1: The Foundations

The first book of the Bible is called Genesis. The word "Genesis" means "beginning," and the first three words of the Bible are "In the beginning."

Genesis begins with the *creation* of the universe. The Bible says that the creation took place over six days. You may choose to read for yourself what happened on each of those days (Genesis 1:1-31), but for your reference, here is a summary:

Day 1: Heavens and Earth; Day and night.
Day 2: Sky.
Day 3: Water above (clouds), water below (sea), dry land, vegetation.
Day 4: Sun, moon, stars.
Day 5: Fish and birds.
Day 6: Land animals, man.
Day 7: No creation today; God rested.

The story now focuses on Adam, the very first human. At first, Adam was without sin, and he and God lived in harmony, communicating with each other daily. Adam was put in a garden, called the Garden of Eden, and was allowed to live there. He was given jobs to do, but all in all he had an easy life.

After some period of time, Adam became lonely, and he asked God for a companion. God had compassion for Adam, and He gave him Eve, the first woman. For a while, Adam and Eve lived just as Adam did in the beginning: in harmony with God, communicating with Him daily.

At this point in human history, everything was perfect. There was no death; if Adam & Eve hadn't done what happens next, they would still be living, to this very day. There was no such thing as embarrassment; Adam and Eve went around naked, and they didn't even notice. There was no pain. For food, all Adam and Eve had to do was grab a piece of fruit from a tree. God had placed several trees in the Garden of Eden, and He told Adam & Eve that they could eat from any of them, *except one*. And that's where things start getting bad.

The one tree that God had forbidden Adam & Eve to eat from was the *Tree of Knowledge of Good and Evil*. Now, keep in mind that the word "knowledge" in this phrase doesn't mean what you think it does. Let me explain.

It's possible to know something, in your mind, by knowing facts about it. But the way the word "knowledge" is used here, it means something more. It means being personally familiar with something. For example, one of my favorite sports stars is a man named Ryne Sandberg, who played second base for the Chicago Cubs in the 1980's and 1990's. I know Ryne Sandberg because I've watched him play, I've read about him, I've read his book, etc. But I've never met him, or eaten dinner with him, or talked to him, or gotten to know his family, or anything like that. So even though I know facts about Ryne Sandberg, I don't *know* him.

So to eat from the Tree of Knowledge of Good and Evil, placed in the center of the Garden of Eden, was to know good and evil not by knowing facts about good and evil, but by being personally familiar with good and evil. God didn't want Adam and Eve to know about evil, but He also wanted them to have that choice (Bible scholars call this "free will.")

Now the Serpent enters the story. The Devil took the form of a serpent (snake), and he entered the Garden of Eden and he tempted Eve. He told her that God was keeping them from that tree because He (God) didn't want them to be like Him. In short, he deceived her because he wanted her to disobey God. Eve took a bite from the fruit of the forbidden tree, and then gave Adam a bite. This was the point at which sin, and its companion, death, entered the world.

This is the first turning point in human history. Remember a few paragraphs ago where I said that, prior to this, everything was perfect? From this point forward in history, nothing would ever again be perfect. The natural order that God created began to decay at that very second, and the decay continues to this day. Living things (humans, plants, animals) grow old, get sick, and die, because of Adam & Eve's sin. You will grow old and die, or maybe even get sick and die at a young age, because of Adam & Eve's sin. Worst yet, Adam & Eve (and every human who has lived on Earth since them) are now, because of sin, separated from God. That daily harmony with God is no more; because of sin, we can no longer be in the presence of God.

But, even as all of this was taking place, God had a plan. Even though sin and death had now entered the world, God had a plan to make everything right. Through His son Jesus, who would enter the world centuries later, the sins of Adam & Eve (and the rest of the world) would be taken away, and through Jesus we would have the power to overcome death, and rise again after death to live forever in Heaven with God. That's the good news, and we'll learn more about that later in this book. But for now, back to the bad news (I'm sorry!).

Because of their sin, God banished Adam & Eve from the Garden. The Bible says they were sent to a place "east of Eden" (Genesis 3:24), and that an angel with a flaming sword guarded the entrance to the Garden, keeping them from ever entering it again. Adam & Eve were banished to the wide open spaces of the world, where Adam & his descendants would have to commit to the hard work of farming the land in order to make a living.

So where was the Garden of Eden? Nobody knows, and it's likely that we'll never know. Some scholars have speculated that it was in the eastern portion of Africa, in the country that is now known as Ethiopia. Other scholars have speculated that it was in what is now Iraq.

Adam and Eve had at least three sons (they probably had more, but only three are mentioned by name), and at least two daughters (probably more, but we know they had at least two because the Bible uses the word "daughters" in the plural). Two of those sons were Cain and Abel. In a fit of jealousy, Cain killed Abel and was banished to live on his own in the wilderness. The other son of Adam & Eve that is mentioned by name in the book of Genesis is named Seth; Seth is the ancestor of Noah, who is the ancestor of all living humans (including me and you).

The next major event in Bible history is the story of Noah. You have probably heard the story of Noah and the flood in Sunday School, but in case you've forgotten it, I'll repeat it here. The Bible says that by the time of Noah, the people of the Earth had become wicked and evil, everyone except for Noah and his family. God decided to destroy the world with a flood, saving only Noah and his family, and the animals that Noah saved, by placing them in a giant boat (an ark).

Noah's ark landed on Mt. Ararat (Mt. Ararat is a real mountain that you can see to this day. It's in the modern country of Turkey, and you can see pictures of the mountain on the internet). On the surface of Mt. Ararat, the animals spread back out over all the Earth, and God made a *covenant* (an agreement) with Noah: that God would never again destroy the Earth with a flood. As a symbol of that covenant, God placed a rainbow in the sky (Genesis 9:13); when you see a rainbow in the sky, it is a symbol that God will never again destroy the world with a flood.

Another significant thing that happened after the flood is this: God gave Noah and his family (his sons were Ham, Shem, and Japheth; the names of his wife and daughters were not recorded) permission to eat meat (Genesis 9:3). Prior to this, God only allowed people to eat things that grew from the ground, such as vegetables and grains.

On Mt. Ararat, Noah and his family were given the job of re-populating the Earth. All of the people of the world are descendents of one Noah's three sons; either Ham, Shem, or Japheth. The ancestor from whom Jesus and His group of people were descended is Shem. At one point in the story, Ham offends Noah (it's not necessary at this point to go into how Ham offends his father) and, in a rage, Noah curses Ham and Ham's son, Canaan (CAY-nuhn). Among other things, Noah says "May Canaan become the slave of

Shem" (Genesis 9:26). This curse will be *very* important later in the Old Testament.

The final major event of the first part of the book of Genesis takes place some number of years after the flood. Once again, the Earth had become populated (you can read about who became the father of whom, and who their descendants were, in Genesis 10). This time, the people decided to build a "tower that reaches to Heaven" (Genesis 11:4). God was displeased with this, and so He made it so that they spoke several different languages and couldn't communicate with each other to complete the tower (prior to this they all spoke the same language). The tower in this story is often called the "Tower of Babel" or the "Tower of Babylon" (BAB-uh-lawn).

Chapter 11 of Genesis concludes the first part of the story, when the foundations of the world were laid. After the Tower of Babel, Chapter 11 provides a few more lists of names and places, and then concludes by telling us about a man named Terah, his grandson Lot, his son Abram, and Abram's wife, Sarai. Abram, Lot and Sarai are the first of the major players in the next part of the book of Genesis, which focuses solely on Abram, his family and servants, and his descendants. Abram, his family, and his descendants are known as the *Patriarchs*.

PART 2: THE PATRIARCHS

The word Patriarch (PAY-tree-ark) comes from two Latin words. The "patri-" part comes from a Latin word that means "father," and the "-arch" part comes from a Latin word that means "ruler." So we can think of the word Patriarch as meaning "father-ruler." And that is how we can think of Abram and his earliest descendants: as the father-rulers of the Jews (don't worry, we'll get into what this means in a moment). Even as late as the last few pages of the New Testament, Abram and his earliest descendants are referred to as the Patriarchs. The time in which Abram and his descendants lived, and the things that happened in those days, are referred to as the Time of the Patriarchs.

The story of the Patriarchs is the story of God building a relationship with a special group of people. God wanted a group of people to be His "chosen people," a group of people that would worship Him and obey His laws. They would have a special relationship with Him, and He would provide for them and protect them, as long as they continued to worship Him and obey Him. And, God would give them a special place where they could live; the Bible calls it the Promised Land.

Before we go any further, now would be a good time to explain the different names God uses to identify His people, because the story of God's relationship with His people begins with Abram. God tells Abram that He

(God) will make a *nation* out of his descendants. The word "nation" in this sentence actually means three things:

1. A *political* nation. In much the same way that the United States of America is a nation with boundaries, its own government, etc., the nation that would eventually be called Israel (more on that in a few pages) was a nation with boundaries, its own government, etc. This nation is called Israel (IZZ-ray-el), and its people are called Israelites (IZZ-ray-el-ites).
2. An *ethnic* nation. What this means is that God's people would all share the same ancestors (Abram and the other Patriarchs) and would share the same blood; they would not marry and have children with foreigners. The people who claim Abram and the Patriarchs as their ancestors would be called Hebrews (HEE-brews).
3. A *religious* nation. God expected His people to worship Him and obey His laws. Their religion is known as Judaism (JOO-day-ism), and the people who practice the religion of Judaism are known as Jews.

All of this is important because, several thousand years after Abram, Jesus was born in Israel. He was a Jew; He practiced the religion of Judaism. He and His people were Hebrews. So, to understand who Jesus was, we need to understand how His people, and how His religion, came to be. The first part of those stories is told here in Genesis, and they begin where we left off: with Abram.

Abram was a wealthy man who lived in the ancient city of Ur (most scholars believe that Ur was in what is now Iraq). It was common in those days for people to move around from place to place for various reasons, and Abram was no exception. It was in a place called Haran that God called Abram, telling him that "I will make you a great nation…all the peoples on Earth will be blessed through you." (Genesis 12:2-3). He also tells Abram that He will (eventually) give him a land that he and his descendants can call their own. God refers to this land as the "Promised Land."

After his calling, several things involving Abram and his family took place. It's not necessary to get into all of them, but here is a brief summary.

1. Abram and his family move from place to place. Abram is unable to move to the Promised Land, at least not right away, because the descendants of Canaan live there.
2. Abram is involved in a couple of military battles.
3. Two cities, Sodom (SAH-dum) and Gomorrah (guh-MORE-uh) are destroyed for being wicked. Abram and his family barely escape,

and Lot's wife disobeys God's command to not turn back and is turned into a pillar of salt for turning to look at the city one last time (Genesis 19:26).

4. Abram fathers a son through his wife's maid (this was a common practice in Abram's day). This son was named Ishmael (ISH-may-el). Today, people who practice the religion of Islam claim that Ishmael is their ancestor. Although Ishmael's name is mentioned a couple of other times in the Old Testament, the story does not focus on him. Instead, it continues with another boy born to Abram: Isaac.

5. God changes Abram's name to Abraham (this name is probably much more familiar to you), and changes Sarai's name to Sarah.

6. Abraham fathers a son through his wife, Sarah. His name is Isaac. Isaac is the next Patriarch, and the Bible continues with his story after Abraham dies.

7. God makes a covenant with Abraham: the Covenant of Circumcision (Genesis 17:11). God tells Abraham that he, and all of his male descendants, must be circumcised, and that this will be a sign of God's relationship with His people. Thousands of years after Abraham, Jewish boys (including Jesus) were (and still are) circumcised because of this covenant. (It's best if you ask a parent or a youth leader what circumcision means.)

8. Abraham and his family are eventually able to live in the Promised Land, though they share it with the descendants of Canaan, the Canaanites (CAY-nuh-nites).

9. God asks Abraham to sacrifice Isaac, as a test to see if he is really obedient to God and really trusts Him. Abraham goes through with the sacrifice, and God spares Isaac's life at the last possible second (Genesis 22:1-18).

Shortly after Abraham tries to sacrifice Isaac, the story moves from Abraham to the second Patriarch, Abraham's son Isaac. Beginning in chapter 24, we learn how Isaac fell in love with his wife, Rebekah, and was allowed to marry her.

Isaac and Rebekah had twin sons, Esau (EE-saw) and Jacob. Esau was born first, and according to the custom of the time, he should have inherited everything from Isaac: his money, his land, his servants, even the blessings of God. However, Jacob tricked Esau (Genesis 25:29-34), and all of these things would instead go to him. Later in the story, Jacob tricks his father Isaac into promising him the blessing that should have been Esau's (27:1-40).

Abraham and Isaac each had other children, sons and daughters, and from those sons and daughters many other tribes and nations would build up.

However, the nation of Israel, God's people, are all descended from Abraham, through Isaac, through Jacob.

The story now moves to Jacob. Because of his trickery, Jacob fled from the Promised Land, fearing that his brother Esau would take his life. Eventually, Jacob marries two women, Leah and Rachel (it was not uncommon at this time in history for a man to have more than one wife).

Before all was said and done in Jacob's life, several things would happen:

First, he and God would wrestle (God took the form of a man for this); because he wrestled with God, he would change his name to Israel (the word Israel means "wrestles with God.") The people of Israel would take the name of their country from Jacob's new name.

Second, through trickery and deceit, often fleeing for his life, Jacob would eventually make his way back to the Promised Land. (It's not necessary to go into all of the things that Jacob did).

Third, and most importantly, Jacob would have several children, from his wives and from his wives' female servants (again, a man having children through his wife's servants was not uncommon at this time in history). Jacob had both sons and daughters. However, as was the custom of the day, the sons were considered the most important. Jacob had twelve sons, and each of those sons would be the ancestor of a tribe. These sons are known as the Twelve Tribes of Israel, and later in the Bible an Israelite's tribe would be very important. The sons/tribes are:

Reuben (ROO-ben)
Simeon (SIM-ee-uhn)
Levi (LEE-vie)
Judah (JOO-duh)
Dan
Naphtali (NAFF-tuh-lee)
Gad
Asher
Issachar (ISS-uh-car)
Zebulon (ZEB-you-luhn)
Joseph
Benjamin

Up until the time of Jesus, every Jew who had ever lived (excluding a very small number of foreigners who had converted to Judaism) was descended from one of Jacob/Israel's 12 sons. Jesus himself was a member of the tribe of Judah. If you really want to impress your parents and youth leaders, you can memorize the names of the twelve tribes, but it isn't really necessary.

The story now moves to the fourth and final Patriarch, Jacob's son Joseph. As a child and young man, Joseph and his brothers didn't get along, mainly because Jacob favored Joseph. You may recall from Sunday School that Joseph's father gave him a very special coat (Genesis 37:3). Joseph also had the power to interpret dreams, and had the power to have dreams that see into the future. Unfortunately for Joseph, he often had dreams in which his brothers would bow to him and serve him.

When Joseph's brothers got tired of him, they made it look like he had died (so they could tell their father that he was dead) and they sold him into slavery. He wound up as a slave in Egypt, but he was lucky: he wound up being the slave of a man named Potiphar (POT-ih-fur) who was very good to him, and who was a servant of the Pharaoh (FAIR-oh), the king of Egypt. Eventually Joseph was put in charge of Potiphar's business and household.

After Potiphar's wife falsely accused Joseph of doing something bad to her, Joseph was put in prison. However, even in prison, God gave Joseph great success, and the prison warden put him in charge of the prison. While there, word got to Pharaoh that Joseph could interpret dreams. Since Pharaoh himself was having some troubling dreams, he called for Joseph.

When Joseph interpreted the dreams for Pharaoh, he told him that seven good years of harvest were coming, but after that there would be seven years of severe famine (a famine is when no food grows and people go hungry and starve to death). He told the Pharaoh to store grain up from each of the good years, so when the famine came there would be food for the people to eat.

Pharaoh was so impressed with Joseph that he put Joseph in charge of all of Egypt. Everyone was to do as Joseph said, and Joseph would be the king's right-hand man. Joseph commanded the Egyptians to do as he told them – to put food into storage for when the famine came.

When the famine did come, Joseph was proved right: storing up the food from the good years was the right thing to do, because now the people had food to eat. The famine was so bad that it affected other parts of the world as well, and people from throughout the world came to Egypt to buy grain to eat. Even Joseph's father and brothers, back in the land of Canaan (remember, Joseph's father Jacob thought Joseph was dead, and his brothers had forgotten about him), were starving. Jacob sent ten of his remaining sons (Benjamin stayed at home) to Egypt to buy food.

Without going into all of the details, over the next few chapters in Genesis we learn about how Joseph provided for his brothers, his father, and their families with Egypt's grain, how he revealed himself to his brothers, and how he convinced his father, Jacob, to bring the family to Egypt. And that is where the story ends, in Egypt. Jacob, his sons and daughters, the sons and daughters of the sons and daughters, all their servants – everyone – came to Egypt to live with Joseph under Pharaoh's care.

This was the beginning of the nation of Israel: one large family of an old man, his twelve sons, many daughters, and all of their children and grandchildren, and all of their servants, a few hundred people total, living in Egypt. Jacob died in Egypt and, on his deathbed, asked to be buried back in the Promised Land. Joseph obeyed his father's wish and buried his father in the land of Canaan. Some time later Joseph died, and his remains were placed in a coffin in Egypt. And that is where the book of Genesis ends.

CHAPTER THREE

OLD TESTAMENT LAW PART 2: THE EXODUS

The word *exodus* means a journey away from a place, and this is what happens in the books of Exodus and Numbers: the Israelites' journey out of Egypt.

Exodus

The book of Exodus begins about 400 years after the death of Joseph. In Genesis, Joseph and his family achieved great wealth, were treated with respect, and were powerful officials in Egypt. When Exodus begins, however, things were different. The Pharaoh who took over after the Pharaoh of Joseph's time died was unkind to the Hebrews, and he feared them. He made them slaves of the Egyptians, and by the time the main story in Exodus begins, the Hebrews have been slaves in Egypt for centuries. Also by this time, the number of Hebrews has grown from a few hundred to around a million or so.

The Pharaoh, in an attempt to limit the size of the Hebrew nation, made a law that all baby boys born to Hebrew women were to be thrown into the Nile river. However, the Egyptian midwives (a midwife is a woman who assists another woman when she's giving birth) refused to do this. One of the Hebrew babies was placed in a basket in the Nile to hide him from the Egyptians. He was found by Pharaoh's daughter, and Pharaoh's daughter named him Moses and decided to raise him as her son. Fortunately for Moses (who was from the tribe of Levi), Pharaoh's daughter hired Moses' actual mother to breast-feed him; so baby Moses got to spend time with his birth mother, his birth mother got paid for spending time with her son, and Moses was raised by royalty.

Little is known about Moses' childhood. It's obvious that Moses knew that he was a Hebrew (Exodus 2:11) and that, even though he was part of Egyptian royalty, the Egyptians knew he was a Hebrew (Exodus 2:15). However, by the time he was a grown man, he had grown to take pity on his people. Early in chapter two, Moses kills an Egyptian for beating a Hebrew. When his crime is found out, Moses flees to a land called Midian. It was while Moses was in Midian that God began to use Moses to finally free His people from slavery.

While in Midian, God spoke to Moses through a burning bush, telling him that God was going to use Moses to free His people. Moses, naturally, wasn't excited about this idea, and offered God several excuses as to why he couldn't do it and God should send someone else (mostly it was because Moses was afraid and didn't fully trust God). Even after God promised to give the Egyptians several signs of His power, Moses still wanted no part of it. Eventually God agreed to have Moses' brother Aaron speak for Moses, while Moses used his staff (a sort of walking stick) to show signs of God's power.

Moses went to the leaders of the Israelites and told them that God was going to free them from slavery. However, Moses' first attempt to get Pharaoh to free them didn't succeed, and Pharaoh responded by making their slavery worse. Moses made a second attempt, this time turning his staff into a snake in front of Pharaoh to show God's power. Pharaoh still refused to let God's people go, so God used ten plagues.

A plague (PLAYG) is an event in which something goes terribly wrong. Usually, it refers to a disease, but it can also refer to an event where something ordinary becomes something terrible. In the book of Exodus, God sends ten plagues; each plague was sent to show God's power and to frighten Pharaoh into letting God's people go. After each of the plagues, Pharaoh refused to let God's people go, though on a few of them he did promise but then later changed his mind.

The plagues are: the plague of blood, where all of the water in the Nile river is turned to blood; the plague of frogs, where tens of millions of frogs jumped out of the ponds and rivers and became so thick that the people of Egypt couldn't walk a step without stepping on them and killing them; the plague of gnats, where hundreds of millions of little bugs tormented the people and animals of Egypt; the plague of flies, where the same thing happened as with the gnats; the plague of livestock, where all of the farm animals (horses, donkeys, sheep, etc.) of the Egyptians died; the plague of boils, where all the Egyptians were covered with painful boils (a boil is like a pimple the size of a grape); the plague of hail, where hail fell from the sky and destroyed the crops and killed everyone who wasn't inside (hail is chunks of ice that fall during bad storms); the plague of locusts, where swarms of giant, biting bugs destroyed all the crops that were in bloom; and the plague of darkness, where for three days there was darkness so thick that no one in Egypt (except the Israelites) could see their hand in front of their face.

The tenth and final plague was the one that finally did the trick and convinced Pharaoh to let God's people go. It is called the plague of the firstborn; in this plague, the first child born to every parent, even the first born animals, would die. At midnight, an Angel of Death would sweep through Egypt, killing all of the firstborn. However, God also provided protection for the Israelites; they were to take a lamb and sacrifice it to God. Then, with the blood of the lamb, they were to make a mark on their door. Any time the angel saw a door with a mark on it, he would *pass over* that house and move on to the next, killing the firstborn in that house.

This event, the *Passover* of the Angel of Death, would go on to become an important (in fact, the most important) feast for the Jews. Every year after that, for thousands of years, up to Jesus' day and even still today, Jews remember the Passover with a feast, remembering how God spared them from death that night, and how God rescued them from Egypt. Each year, the Jews would sacrifice a lamb in honor of the Passover (Jews no longer do this, though they still celebrate Passover, just in a different way).

In much the same way, we Christians can think of Jesus as our Passover lamb. In fact, one of the names for Jesus in the New Testament is the Lamb of God. By dying for us on the cross (and spilling His blood), and taking away our sins, Jesus' blood spares us from death (by allowing us to live forever with Him in Heaven after we die) just like the blood of the Passover lamb spared the Israelites from death in Egypt.

God had given instructions to the Israelites before the plague of the firstborn was to take place. He warned them that they would have to leave in the middle of the night, on a moment's notice, when He gave the command. They had been instructed to ask their Egyptian neighbors for donations of gold and silver (the Bible says that ordinary Egyptians – not the slave drivers or Egyptian royalty, but regular people - were kind to their Hebrew neighbors); they had to prepare their meals just so*; they had to prepare their houses, livestock and belongings just so; even the way they wore the clothes on their backs had to be just right, in preparation for God's command to leave Egypt in a hurry.

*God gave the Israelites instructions to prepare dough for bread, but without yeast (yeast is what helps make bread rise and taste light and fluffy), so it would be ready when they left Egypt in a hurry. The process of yeast making bread rise is called *leavening*; and since the Israelites left Egypt without putting yeast in their bread, one of the other names for Passover is the Feast of the Unleavened Bread.

On God's command, the Israelites left Egypt in the middle of the night, with Moses leading them. God led them with a "pillar of cloud" by day and a "pillar of fire" by night (Exodus 13:21). After a few days, they had made their way to the Red Sea (or possibly a smaller body of water in the Middle East), when the Egyptians decided to pursue them. With Pharaoh's men coming after them from the west, and the sea to the east, the people became terrified and started to doubt God. But Moses, using God's power, caused the water of the sea to separate to make room for them to pass. Once the Israelites were on the other side, and the Egyptians were catching up to them, God caused the waters to return to normal, drowning the Egyptians.

Throughout the next few chapters of the book of Exodus, a pattern begins. The people of Israel will find themselves in a difficult situation (for example, they're running out of water; they're running out of food, etc.); they'll grumble and complain about Moses and Aaron's leadership; they'll wish they were back in Egypt; Moses will scold them; and God will provide for them in miraculous ways.

One of the ways in which God provided for the people during this time was by giving them a type of bread called *manna* (MAN-nuh). Every morning, the ground would be covered by a sweet, white, flaky bread that was unlike anything the Israelites had ever seen before. God provided just enough for each person to eat every day. He warned the people that they should trust Him and not save some for the next day, because there would be no need. Those who did take too much found out the next day that the bread they saved had gone rotten. In Exodus 16:32, God commands Moses and Aaron to save some manna and place it in a jar, so that the people of Israel will remember manna, and remember God providing for them, once they reached the Promised Land.

When they reached Mt. Sinai (SYE-nye), God called Moses to come to the top of the mountain so He could give instructions to Moses, and so He (God) could reveal Himself to the people. While on the top of Mt. Sinai, God gave Moses ten laws for the people to follow. Those laws are known as the Ten Commandments (Exodus 20:1-17). God also gave Moses, with instructions to give to the people, several other laws in addition to the Ten Commandments. In Chapter 4, we'll talk about the Ten Commandments, and about the rest of the laws that are given in the first five books of the Old Testament.

Some of the laws given to Moses on Mt. Sinai involved how God was to be worshipped while the people were in the desert. God commanded the people to make a special, portable building that would be used as a temporary house of worship until a temple could be built in the Promised Land. This temporary temple was called the *Tabernacle* (TAB-er-nack-uhl), and chapters

25-30 describe, in exact detail, how the Tabernacle and the things inside it were to be made and used.

One of the things to be placed in the Tabernacle is known as the Ark of the Covenant. This was supposed to be a special container that would hold objects from Israel's history and remind them of their journey out of slavery. The Ark was a very special and very important part of the Jews' worship, and it plays a role in a couple of military battles later on in the Bible.

While Moses was on Mt. Sinai, receiving the law from God, the people began, once again, to get restless and to complain about Moses. This time, they drew Aaron into their complaint. They asked Aaron to make an idol for them that they could worship instead of God. Aaron asked them to donate their gold jewelry, melted down the gold, and made a golden calf for the people to worship. Needless to say, God was quite unhappy about this, and when Moses asked Aaron about it, Aaron lied and said that the people threw their gold into the fire, and the calf came out!

Exodus ends with God punishing the people for worshipping the golden calf, then goes on to give a few more pages of laws (which we will talk about in Chapter 4).

NUMBERS

The title of the book of Numbers refers to the fact that two censuses were taken while the people were waiting to enter the Promised Land. A census is when a government makes a count of all the people living in a country. In the book of Numbers, God commanded Moses to record how many people were in the nation of Israel, and who their tribal leaders were, before they could enter the Promised Land. Much of the book of Numbers is lists of names, and another large part of it is a list of laws. The rest of it, the part we will focus on here, is the final part of the story of the journey out of Egypt and into the Promised Land.

The pattern of the people grumbling and getting into trouble, of Moses scolding them, and of God providing for them, continues into the book of Numbers. Along the way, the Israelites encountered foreigners who tempted some of the people into worshipping foreign gods; into marrying foreign women; or both. Throughout the journey, God shows remarkable patience for His people, even though they don't deserve it.

Now would be a good time to talk about just what is meant by the words "Promised Land." All the way back in Abraham's day, God had promised that He would provide for His people a land that they could call their own. He sometimes described it as a land "flowing with milk and honey." It would be a land that they could farm (which was vitally important to a people used to living in a desert). By the time the people arrived there, each tribe would have its own section to claim as their own (more on that in Chapter 4).

To get an idea of where the Promised Land was, you need to look no further than a map of the modern day nation of Israel. Find one in your Bible, or look on the Internet. The little strip of land between the Jordan river on the east, and the Mediterranean Sea on the west, was the land that God promised to His people, where they would live (with a couple of breaks) for over a thousand years, right up through Jesus' time.

You will see that, to the south and west of the Promised Land, is Egypt, and to the north and east of the Promised Land is the modern-day nation of Iraq. In Bible times Egypt was a powerful nation, and the nations to the north and east (which went by different names throughout Bible history) were equally powerful nations. To travel between those two nations, the only way to go was along the narrow stretch of land that God promised to His people (the other way was through several hundred miles of desert, which was all but impossible). This was important, because God placed His people where they could have influence on foreigners and be examples of what it means to worship God to the whole world. Unfortunately, it didn't exactly work out that way, but we'll talk more about that in Chapter 5.

You'll also recall that, way back in Noah's time, God had said that Canaan would be the slave of Shem (see page 15 of this book). This is important, because when the Israelites (Shem's descendants) arrived at the entrance to the Promised Land after their journey from Egypt, the land was settled by Canaanites (Canaan's descendants), and had been for hundreds, if not thousands, of years. In Abraham's day, he and as his family, as well as the families of Isaac and Jacob, lived there as foreigners. However, now the whole nation of Israel (around a million people) was ready to live in the land, and to make that happen, the Canaanites would have to go.

The story of the Exodus picks up again in Numbers 13. As the people are nearing the Promised Land, God commands Moses to send spies, one from each of the twelve tribes, to scout out the Canaanites' land, see what is there, and report back. The twelve spies did as they were told, exploring the land for forty days, and brought back their report. Only two spies, Caleb and Joshua, believed that God would give them the land, like He had promised. The rest were afraid of the Canaanites and tried to convince the Israelites to return to Egypt.

Because of their sin of not believing that God would fulfill His promises to them, and of plotting to return to Egypt, Moses, Aaron, the unbelieving spies, and the whole nation of Israel were punished. God declared that they would wander in the desert for forty years (one year for each day the spies explored) until they had all died. Only Caleb, Joshua, and those who were nineteen years old or younger at the time of the spy mission, would live to see the Promised Land.

As they wandered through the desert (getting into various military battles at times), the people continued the pattern that I mentioned earlier: getting into unpleasant situations, grumbling against Moses, God providing, etc. This pattern continued for forty years, until Moses died and the people were ready to enter the Promised Land, under Joshua's leadership. We'll resume the story of the entry into the Promised Land, and what happened afterwards, as we discuss the twelve books of Old Testament history in Chapter 5. If you would like to continue reading the history of the Old Testament, you can skip straight to Chapter 5.

CHAPTER FOUR

OLD TESTAMENT LAW PART 3: THE LAWS

Even though I referred to the first five books of the Old Testament as the books of Law, much of it (as you have learned from reading the two previous chapters) is actually historical narrative. The rest, however, is actual law. That is, several hundred pages of these five books are lists of laws that God gave to the people. Of the book of Exodus, about a third of it contains laws; Leviticus, almost all of it; Numbers, a little more than half; and Deuteronomy, almost all of it.

God's laws for His people begin with the Ten Commandments, given to Moses on Mt. Sinai in Exodus 20. If you want to impress your parents and youth leaders, memorize the Ten Commandments. Here is a summary of the Ten Commandments (they are not written word-for-word here; this is just a summary), and after that we'll talk about what they mean.

1. You must have no other gods before me (God).
2. You must not make idols or worship images.
3. You must not misuse God's name.
4. Remember the Sabbath day, and keep it holy.
5. Honor your father and your mother.
6. You must not commit adultery.
7. You must not commit murder.
8. You must not steal.
9. You must not give false testimony against your neighbor.
10. You must not covet your neighbor's belongings.

Now that you know what the commandments are, let's talk about what they mean.

1. **You must have no other gods before me (God)**. There is only one God. The name of God as it is written in the Old Testament is Yahweh; today most English-speaking Christians just call Him "God," and that's OK. His name is not Baal or Ashtoreth (two foreign gods that people in Bible times worshipped), or Allah or Vishnu (two gods that non-Christians worship today). We must only worship God.

2. **You must not make idols or worship images**. An idol is an object, usually something carved out of wood or stone, or made of metal, that people worship. In Bible times idol worship was quite common. In your life, you can think of an idol as anything that becomes more important than God in your life. Perhaps a video game, or a friend, or a TV show – anything that takes the place of God in your life is an idol.

3. **You must not misuse God's name**. God's name is special, and so it should be treated with respect. Saying things like "Oh my God" or "I swear to God…" dishonors God's name.

4. **Remember the Sabbath day, and keep it holy**. God commanded His people to take a day of rest every seventh day, and to not do any work on that day. This day is called the Sabbath Day. Jews (both in Bible times and in modern times) believe that the Sabbath begins at sundown on the sixth day (Friday) and lasts until sundown on Saturday. We Christians, on the other hand, have made Sunday our Sabbath Day, and we follow the Roman method of starting a new day at midnight. Church historians will tell you that Christians began treating Sunday as the Sabbath Day because it is the day on which Jesus rose from the dead. NOTE: Read the footnote at the end of this section for some more discussion about the Sabbath Day as it relates to Christians.

5. **Honor your father and your mother**. Your parents deserve to be treated with respect and honor, and you should obey them and do what they ask you to do.

6. **You must not commit adultery**. You should probably ask your parents to explain to you what this commandment means in more detail. But in general, it means that you should not have a marriage relationship with someone who you are not married to.

7. **You must not commit murder**. Some translations say "you must not kill," but that's not the correct meaning of this commandment. Killing another person is allowed, but only in self-defense (or

in defense of someone who can't defend their self), in war, or as punishment for certain crimes; to kill another person otherwise is to commit murder.

8. **You must not steal**. You must not take something that doesn't belong to you without paying for it or without the owner's permission.
9. **You must not give false testimony against your neighbor**. This is a fancy way of saying that you must not lie.
10. **You must not covet your neighbor's belongings**. This means that you shouldn't hate someone for having something that you want. God wants you to be satisfied with what you have, and if you want something, to earn it.

NOTE ABOUT THE SABBATH DAY: There is some debate about what this commandment means to Christians. Many Christians believe that in order to honor God, we must not do any work on Sunday. This means no mowing the lawn, no doing homework, not even pumping gas. There are even some Christians who insist that this commandment should be followed in the Old Testament way, meaning that work should stop on Friday night and not start again until Saturday night. However, Hebrews 4 teaches us that Jesus is our Sabbath-rest. In other words, because of Jesus, we are no longer required to have a special day where no work is done; Jesus Himself is our rest. The exact meaning of this passage is debated by Bible scholars, but my opinion (and my opinion is shared by a lot of Bible scholars and Christian leaders) is that you should go to church and worship God on Sundays, and try to make Sunday a special day of serving God, but you shouldn't make too big a deal about the not working part and inconvenience yourself by going out of your way do avoid doing work.

After the Ten Commandments, God proceeds to give several hundred other laws over the course of the books of Exodus, Leviticus, Numbers and Deuteronomy. Some of these laws are very specific, even dealing with such things as how you should treat burns on the skin!

Rather than talk about all of the Old Testament laws, or even give a sample of them, it would be best to talk about the laws in various categories. This will give you a better understanding of what the laws were really about, and what they mean for the rest of the Bible.

1. **Ceremonial Laws.** These laws cover how the people are to worship God. They cover how they are to prepare themselves for worship, how they are to conduct themselves during worship, how they are to sacrifice, etc. These laws were relevant to Judaism and are not relevant to Christians today.*

2. **Civil Laws.** In the same way that the United States of America has laws that cover how people are to treat each other, how business is conducted, etc., ancient Israel also had laws that dealt with matters of government, property, crime, business, etc.

3. **Geographical Laws.** You may remember from school that geography is the study of places on maps. In the book of Numbers, each tribe of Israel was to be given a certain area within the Promised Land where they could live. Every tribe except Levi and Joseph (for reasons that I'll get into in a moment) had their own land. Joseph's tribe was split into two tribes, named after his sons, Ephraim and Manasseh, and each of those two tribes got their own section of the Promised Land. Levi did not get a section – see why in the note at the end of this chapter.

4. **Household Laws.** These laws described how people were to treat diseases; the clothes they could wear; how they could treat their slaves; how families were to interact with each other; who could marry whom; and similar issues.

5. **Laws of Clean & Unclean/Dietary Laws.** These laws described what the Jews could eat ("clean" animals) and not eat ("unclean" animals); how they were to prepare and store their food; animals, people, and things that they were to regard as "clean" (meaning they could touch, use, interact with, etc.) and "unclean" (meaning they could not touch, use, interact with, etc.).

6. **Sabbath Laws.** These laws described what could and could not be done on the Sabbath day. Basically any kind of activity that could be remotely considered "work" (such as starting a fire) was forbidden.

By the time Jesus came, most Jews were routinely breaking many of the laws. In fact, in Jesus' time the Jewish leaders believed that for one to truly be a Jew, they had to obey only the Sabbath Laws and the Laws of Clean and Unclean. And the Jewish leaders of Jesus' time took those laws *very* seriously, to the point that they forbade people from doing things that weren't even forbidden in the Old Testament, simply out of fear that they might break the law unintentionally. This will be important in the New Testament, because a lot of what Jesus did upset the Jewish leaders of His day because they believed He was violating their laws.

If you decide to read some of the laws of the Old Testament, you may start to feel guilty because you've broken some of them. In fact, you've probably broken a lot of them in your life, or even today. If you are wearing a garment that is made of two kinds of fabric, you've violated an Old Testament law. If you've eaten pork, you've violated an Old Testament law. If you've eaten a cheeseburger, you've violated Old Testament law.

But don't worry – you're not doing anything wrong by violating Old Testament law. When Jesus came, He made it clear that, because of Him, the Law was no longer necessary. When He died on the cross, He took with Him the sin of the world, and with that sin, the Law. As a Christian, you are not a slave to the Law, and instead, you live under a law of grace (Romans 6:14).

Most Christian leaders believe that the only laws Christians need to follow are laws that are given, or repeated, in the New Testament. This means that Christians must obey the Ten Commandments, plus some other instructions that the New Testament gives. We'll talk about those later in this book. And remember, even if you break God's law and sin against Him, if you are a Christian your sins are forgiven, and you live under God's grace.

So why was the law so specific, complicated, and difficult to follow? That's a matter of debate, but most Bible scholars will point to the fact that God wanted His people to be holy – and in this case, the word "holy" just means "unique" or "different." God's people were to be separate from the other people of the world, and to do that meant giving them different ways of dressing, different ways of eating, different ways of dealing with one another, etc., from the rest of the people of the world. By keeping His people different from the rest of the world, they would be more focused on God and more likely to worship only Him. Unfortunately, it didn't work out that way, but we'll read more about that later in this book.

Also, by making the Law so complicated, it was all but impossible for a person to follow every word of it, every day of their lives. In fact, many Bible scholars believe that God designed the Law so that no one would be able to live their life without breaking it – because, by breaking the Law, a person has committed sin and needs to be saved. And every person on Earth can be saved through God's son, Jesus.

*Even though it's not relevant to Christian worship, there is an aspect of Jewish Ceremonial Law that is important for you to learn, because it will come up in the New Testament. Among all of the rules and regulations for worship, God set apart the people of the tribe of Levi, called Levites (LEE-vites) to perform certain duties related to worship. Some of the descendants of Levi, who were also descendants of Aaron, were given the job of priests, and they had specific duties related to worship as well. It's not important to get into what those duties were, but do remember the words "priests" and "Levites," and what they mean, because they will come up in the New Testament. Because the Levites were given specific instructions about where they could live, they did not get their own section of the Promised Land.

CHAPTER FIVE

OLD TESTAMENT HISTORY

The twelve books of Old Testament history tell us the story of how the Israelites entered the Promised Land and what happened after they finally settled there. These books cover a period of about a thousand years, and cover the time from the very beginnings of the nation of Israel (a political nation), through their high points as a dominant world power, through their low points worshipping idols and being punished by being carried off into slavery, and then the re-establishment of the nation after returning from slavery. That's a lot to cover, so let's get started.

You'll remember that we left off with the nation of Israel at the entrance to the Promised Land. Joshua is their leader (Moses is dead), and they've been given the Law to guide them and rule them once they enter the land. The land is populated by the descendants of Canaan, but God has told the Israelites that the land is theirs, and they are to drive out the Canaanites.

JOSHUA

The first book of Old Testament History, Joshua, was written (mostly) by Joshua himself and tells the story of the entry into the Promised Land. The story begins with another spy mission (you'll remember that Joshua was one of the spies sent on a spy mission way back in Numbers). The first Canaanite city that needed to be conquered was Jericho, and Joshua sent spies to check it out.

The spies hid out in the house of a woman named Rahab. Rahab told the spies that the people of Jericho were in fear of the Israelites, and knew that they would be killed or driven out because God was with them. However, since Rahab showed kindness to the spies and didn't rat them out to the king of Jericho, the spies agreed to make sure that the Israelites spared the lives of Rahab and her family when they took over Jericho.

On God's command, everyone in Israel crossed the Jordan river, marking their official entry into the Promised Land. God gave specific instructions for the order in which they were to cross the river, and how they were to do it. After crossing the river, it was time to take Jericho.

Jericho, like most cities of the day, was surrounded by a wall. In ancient history, cities were generally surrounded by thick walls to keep invaders out. These walls had gates that people could come and go through if they had business inside or outside the city, but otherwise the walls kept people out. Jericho's walls were thick – so thick, said the Israelites, that you could turn a chariot around in a circle on top of the walls. Because of the thick walls, the Israelites feared they wouldn't be able to take the city. But God had a plan: He told them to march around the city for six days; on the seventh day, the priests were to blow their horns, and the people were to shout, and the walls would crumble. The people did as they were told, and the wall crumbled, and Jericho was taken by the Israelites.

The rest of the book of Joshua describes the various military battles in which Israel took over cities and places in the Promised Land. At times, some of the people sinned – for example, Achan, who kept some plundered gold for himself and paid for it with his life (Joshua 7). At other times, God performed miracles to help the Israelites – for example, making the sun stand still in the sky for a day while the Israelites were at battle (Joshua 10:1-15). The Israelites defeated all of the tribes in the land, exactly as they were instructed to, except for a couple of them. One of those tribes was the Philistines, and Israel's failure to drive out the Philistines would come back to haunt them for centuries. The book of Joshua ends with Joshua dying and him, along with his ancestor Jacob, being buried in the Promised Land.

JUDGES

After the death of Joshua, Israel now had almost full control over the Promised Land. You would think that the people would have given their thanks to God by obeying Him completely. Unfortunately, it wasn't so. Not long after Joshua died, the people began worshipping idols and the gods of their neighbors. Each period of idol-worship would lead to a period of slavery; at this time in history, it was not uncommon for nations and tribes to enslave people that they defeated. The people would then repent, and they would be rescued from slavery by a person known as a judge. In this case, a judge is a person who has control of the government, the way a president does today, but who is also a military leader who uses war and battle to free the people.

The book of Judges contains six cycles of Sin (the people worship idols) – Slavery (the people are enslaved by a foreign tribe) – Sorrow (the people realize that they've done wrong and beg God for mercy) – Salvation (God rescues the people and sends judges to save them and rule them) – back to Sin (the people would forget about God saving them and start worshipping idols again).

The last of the judges mentioned in the book of Judges (there was one other judge, who is not mentioned in this book, who we'll talk about later) is named Samson. You may be familiar with the story of Samson and Delilah from Sunday School, but if you're not, I'll summarize it here.

When Samson was born, Israel was enslaved by the Philistines. God told Samson's mother that he (Samson) was never to have his hair cut or have his beard shaved. When he grew up, he was known for his incredible strength, and for his ability to kill his enemies with weak weapons, or with no weapons at all. After Samson killed a thousand Philistines, he was made judge over the Israelites and judged them for twenty years. Unfortunately, Samson fell in love with a Philistine woman (the Israelites were forbidden from having relationships with foreigners) who tricked him into revealing that his power came from his long hair. When he was shaved, his strength left him and he was blinded and imprisoned. As his hair grew back, his strength returned, and in one last act of revenge against the Philistines Samson tore down the Philistine temple to their god, killing himself and several thousand Philistines in the process.

The book of Judges ends with Israel in chaos (chaos means no order), with some of them attacking their own people, from the tribe of Benjamin.

RUTH

The book of Ruth tells the story of one brief incident that happened at some point during the time of the judges. Ruth was the daughter-in-law of Naomi. The women lived in Moab (a foreign country). Because of a drought, both women were in danger of starving. Ruth managed to find work in a barley field near Bethlehem (a town in the Promised Land). As a foreigner, the other field hands could have treated Ruth very poorly. However, the owner of the field (a man named Boaz) took pity on her and gave her an easier job. Eventually Ruth and Boaz married. It is important to note that Ruth had a son, Obed, whose grandson was David, who would become a *very* important figure later on in the Old Testament. Obed was also an ancestor of Jesus.

1 & 2 SAMUEL

These two books tell the story of Samuel, the last judge, and Israel's change from being a nation ruled by judges to a nation ruled by kings. Many times throughout 1 Samuel the people ask for a king, and many times God tells them that they really don't want a king. Under a king the people basically live in slavery, because they have to do whatever the king says and don't have any legal rights. However, the people continued to ask for a king, and eventually they got one. It would be a decision they would grow to regret.

So why did the people want a king? Probably for the same reason that they continued to worship idols, as they did from the time of the judges and would continue to do through the time of the kings: peer pressure. You may hear your parents telling you about peer pressure: that's the need to try to be like your friends and fit in with them. The same thing happened to the Israelites: they wanted to be like the other nations; so they worshipped idols (like the other nations), and they asked for a king (so they could be like the other nations - see 1 Samuel 8:19-20).

But back to Samuel. In those days it was considered a great dishonor for a woman to be unable to have children. Samuel's mother, Hannah, made a promise to God that if she were able to have a son, she would dedicate that son to God. So when Samuel was born, she honored her vow and took him to live with the priest, Eli. As Samuel became a grown man, he made it known to Israel that God was with him, leading Israel through military success and through helping rid the people of some evil priests.

Even with Samuel's wise and honest rule as judge, the people asked for a king. He kept warning them against it, but after they kept asking, God told Samuel to name a king. The man he chose was named Saul. Saul was a powerful military ruler, and the people were on his side, but he was also hot-headed and arrogant. And, at the end of his reign as king, he disobeyed God; God had ordered Saul to attack a city and totally destroy it, but instead Saul kept some of the goods from the city for himself. For this sin, God ordered that Saul could no longer be king, and He made Samuel pick someone else.

This is where David enters the story. Eventually David would become the most powerful of Israel's kings, and a central figure of Judaism (the symbol on the flag of the modern-day nation of Israel is called the "Star of David"). However, at the beginning he was just a regular young man. He was the youngest son of a shepherd, in days when important jobs went to oldest sons first. Samuel knew when he saw him that David should be king. However, David didn't become King right away. Instead, he became a servant in Saul's royal court, and later, in his army.

You may be familiar with the story of David and Goliath (1 Samuel 17) from Sunday School, but in case you aren't, I'll re-tell it here. Israel was once again at war with the Philistines, and this time, they were losing. The Philistines offered a choice: Israel could send one man to fight one Philistine. If Israel's man won, the Philistines would surrender, and if the Philistines' man won, Israel would surrender.

The Philistines' soldier was Goliath, who the Bible describes as being a giant. When no Israelite soldier was brave enough to face him, David took the challenge. With nothing but a sling and a rock, he killed Goliath and forced the terrified Philistines to flee.

When word of David's actions got back to the people, they started praising him and making fun of Saul. Naturally, Saul wasn't happy about this. He grew jealous and tried, several times, to kill David, and David spent much of his early life on the run from Saul.

After several years on the run, and several successful military victories by both Saul and David, Saul took his own life when the Philistines were closing in on him. Shortly after Saul's death, David got word and returned, and was eventually named king over all of Israel.

As I said earlier, David was the most powerful king Israel would have. With David on the throne, Israel was a nation of wealth, power, military strength, and strong rule among the people. With David on the throne, Israel was more powerful than it had ever been, and it would never be as powerful again. But, even as Israel's military power grew, the Philistines continued to go to war with Israel time and time again (remember, I told you that Israel would regret their decision not to drive out the Philistines when they had the chance).

David had a long and interesting life. He started out as the youngest son of a shepherd. He then became a low-ranking soldier in the army. He was also a musician (1 Samuel 16:14-23) and poet; even after he became King, David wrote several songs and poems, several of which are in the book of Psalms. David loved God and worshipped him with everything he had; the Bible describes David as "a man after God's own heart" (2 Samuel 13:14).

However, David had his flaws. His continued military battles had made him a very violent man. In 2 Samuel 11, we read that David got another man's wife pregnant and had her husband sent to the front lines of battle to be killed. David also couldn't control his own sons; one of them, Amnon, committed a terrible crime against his own half-sister. Then his other son, Absalom, killed Amnon in revenge.

1 & 2 Kings and 1 & 2 Chronicles

After David died, his son Solomon became king. You may be familiar with Solomon; he was one of the wealthiest men, and one of the wisest men, who ever lived. He ruled Israel fairly and was known for being a wise ruler. He wrote two books of the Bible (Ecclesiastes and Song of Songs), most or all of another one (Proverbs), and a small part of a fourth (Psalms).

Under Solomon, the Temple was built. You'll remember that, during the Exodus, the Jews worshipped in a portable house of worship known as the Tabernacle. They worshipped in that Tabernacle for centuries. David had wanted to build a temple, so the Jews would have a permanent place to worship, but God wouldn't allow it, because of David's flaws. However, with Solomon on the throne, the Temple was built. It was one of the most magnificent buildings ever built, and Jews worshipped there for centuries (up until shortly after the time of Jesus). Important events in the New Testament took place in the Temple.

I could describe the Temple to you, but it would take several pages, and my words wouldn't be good enough to describe it properly. Instead, you can read what the Bible has to say about the Temple in 1 Kings chapters 5-8.

Today, nothing remains of the Temple except for one stone wall. If you watch the news, you may see modern Jews praying at the one wall that remains at the Temple. If you would like to see what that wall looks like, have a parent help you look it up on the internet. Today it's known as the Wailing Wall.

In spite of his wisdom, near the end of his life Solomon started to get into some bad habits. He began falling in love with foreign women, in spite of God's law not to marry foreigners. Unfortunately, these women convinced Solomon to worship idols. Because of this, God told Solomon that He would "tear the Kingdom" from him after he died (1 Kings 11:11).

And so, after the death of Solomon, we enter a period of Bible history that Bible scholars call the Divided Kingdom (the time of Saul, David and Solomon is known as the United Kingdom). You'll remember that each tribe was given a part of the Promised Land to live in. After Solomon's death, the kingdom split into two. The ten northern tribes kept the name Israel and made the city of Samaria their capital. The two southern tribes (Judah and Simeon) took the name Judah and kept Jerusalem as their capital.

Israel was ruled by nineteen kings, and all of them were evil. Judah was ruled by nineteen kings (and one queen). Some of them were good (though none as good as David), and most of them were evil.

If you want to impress your parents and youth leaders, you can memorize the names of the kings of Judah and Israel. Right now, it's not important to learn a lot of detail about what they did, but you would do well to at least be familiar with their names. As you study the Bible throughout your life, you will have the opportunity to learn more about the actions of the kings of Israel and Judah.

Israel	Judah
Jeroboam I (Jeroboam the First)	Rehoboam (evil)
Nadab	Abijah (evil)
Baasha	Asa (good)
Elah	Jehoshaphat (good)
Zimri	Jehoram (evil)
Omri	Ahaziah (evil)
Ahab	(queen) Athaliah (evil)
Ahaziah	Joash (good)
Jehoram	Amaziah (good)
Jehu	Azariah (also known as Uzziah) (good)
Jehoahaz	Jotham (good)
Jehoash	Ahaz (evil)
Jeroboam II	Hezekiah (good)
Zechariah	Manasseh (the worst)
Shallum	Amon (evil)
Menahem	Josiah (the best)
Pekahiah	Jehoahaz (evil)
Pekah	Jehoiakim (evil)
Hoshea	Jehoiachin (evil)
	Zedekiah (evil)

The books of 1 & 2 Kings tell what happened under the kings of both Israel and Judah, while the books of 1 & 2 Chronicles tell what happened only under the kings of Judah (although Saul, David and Solomon are also discussed in 1 Chronicles).

The time of the Divided Kingdom is an ugly part of the history of God's people. Not only did the kings of Israel (and the evil kings of Judah) worship idols, but they made the people worship idols, too. Some of the kings (of Judah) went so far as put up altars to foreign gods in the Temple.

The people were, in general, treated poorly during this time. Those who chose to follow God were often tortured and put to death. Several times the king's men would commit crimes against the people, just for fun.

Two men are the most important figures in the time of the Divided Kingdom: the prophets Elijah (ee-LYE-juh) and Elisha (ee-LYE-sha). Both men lived during the time of evil kings, and both men tried to convince the kings to do what was right. At times they put their lives in danger by speaking against the kings. During their lives, Elijah and Elisha both performed miracles and helped people who were suffering because of their kings.

After Hoshea, the last king of Israel, the Israelites were enslaved and taken away to a land called Assyria (ass-SEER-ee-uh). This didn't happen all at once: instead, groups of Israelites were taken captive several times, over the course of several years, beginning with kings before Hoshea. The Assyrians took first the wealthiest and most-educated Israelites to be slaves, then the wealthiest and most-educated among who was left, and so on. By the time the Assyrians finished taking slaves, the only Israelites left in Israel were very few people, all of whom were poor, uneducated, and disabled. The period of time when the Israelites were kept in Assyria as slaves is known as the Assyrian (ass-SEER-ee-uhn) Captivity.

After Zedekiah, the last king of Judah, the people of Judah were also enslaved and taken away. The people of Judah were taken to a land called Babylon (BAB-uh-lawn). Like the Israelites and the Assyrians, the captivity of the people of Judah didn't take place all at once; and, a few people remained. Those who stayed behind were also poor, uneducated and disabled. The period of time when the people of Judah were kept as slaves in Babylon is known as the Babylonian (bab-uh-LONE-ee-uhn) Captivity.

The books of Daniel and Esther, which we'll talk about later, give us a look at what life was like for the Jews under captivity. In general, the Jews were treated well by their captors, as long as they did as they were told. Some of the Jews (like Daniel) even became important officials. However, God's people were away from their Promised Land, and what remained of their Promised Land was controlled by foreigners. Eventually, the Jews returned from captivity, little by little, and re-took the Promised Land.

Ezra & Nehemiah

Ezra was a Jew, living in slavery in Babylon, who was descended from Aaron. Since his ancestor was Aaron, he was allowed to be a priest. God moved the heart of the King, Cyrus, to allow the Jews to return to Jerusalem and repair the temple. The book of Ezra gives a detailed summary of the work he and the people did, and the people who came with him, and their descendants.

Nehemiah was also a Jew, living in slavery in Babylon. Even though he was a slave, he was a high-ranking official and trusted friend of the King. Using his position of trust with the king, Nehemiah convinced the king to allow him to bring some Jews back to Jerusalem and re-build the city. The book of Nehemiah gives a detailed summary of the work he and the people did, and also how some of the local officials who had been occupying the Promised Land tried to stop him.

ESTHER

The book of Esther tells the story of an event that happened during the Assyrian captivity. Esther was a Jew who was chosen to be the queen. Esther learned that some of the king's men were planning to kill the Jews. Esther used her position as queen to convince the king not to kill the Jews. Instead, the King gave the Jews permission to kill those who wanted to harm them.

AFTER THE CAPTIVITY

Nehemiah was placed in charge of the people as their governor (not king), and Ezra served as their priest. The Jews had returned to the Promised Land and once again made it their own, thought it was still officially part of the empire of Persia (now modern-day Iran). The history of the Old Testament ends here, and we'll talk about the history between the Old Testament and New Testament in Chapter 7.

CHAPTER SIX

OLD TESTAMENT POETRY AND PROPHECY

The remaining twenty two books of the Old Testament, the books of Poetry, Major Prophets, and Minor Prophets, were written at different times in Old Testament history and involve a lot of people and events that we've learned about in previous chapters.

POETRY

It's best not to think of Old Testament poetry in the same way you think of modern poetry. Old Testament poetry usually didn't rhyme (although some of it did rhyme) and (usually) didn't have a beat, the way modern poetry does. Instead, the poetry of the Old Testament depended on the way the words sounded to the ear, and the way the words described what they were talking about, to make a beautiful poem.

The first book of poetry, Job, is like a diary. A man named Job, who loved God and worshipped him, was also very respected and very wealthy. Job lost everything – his wealth, his family, even his health. The devil believed that, if Job lost everything, he would stop worshipping God. However, Job continued to worship God, and eventually became even wealthier and happier than he was before.

The book records Job's thoughts and prayers as he goes through all of his suffering. The book also records the words of some of Job's friends, who gave him advice about how to deal with his suffering. Many Bible scholars consider Job to be a book about how to deal with suffering.

The next book of poetry is Psalms. A psalm is a poem or a song (it can be one or the other), and 150 of them are in this book. Most of them were written by David, but others were written by other authors whose names are given, and many others are anonymous (meaning the author's name is not known).

Some of the Psalms are joyful, some are sad, some are hopeful, and some are downright angry. Some of them relate directly to events in David's life; for example, David wrote Psalm 51 after he felt guilty for getting a woman pregnant and having her husband killed.

The book of Proverbs is a collection of wise sayings, and most of them came from Solomon. In them, the writer gives advice to the reader about how to live your life wisely. In many of the Proverbs, the writer also talks about things that are foolish to do.

The book of Ecclesiastes is also like a diary. It's a collection of the author's thoughts (the author of most of the book is probably Solomon) as he thinks about things like the meaning of life.

The book of Song of Songs (or Song of Solomon) was written by Solomon. Think of this book as a love poem; it describes the relationship between two people who love each other, and the things they say to each other out of their love for one another.

Major Prophets

Before we talk about the books of the prophets, it's a good idea to talk about what is meant by prophecy (PROF-uh-see) and by being a prophet.

You may think that a prophet is someone who tells what is going to happen in the future. That is true, but only up to a point. One of the most important jobs of a prophet is to tell what is happening *right now*. Throughout the books of Judges, Samuel, Kings, Chronicles, and others, prophets are called by God to tell people (usually the king) about things that are going on at the moment. Usually, it's to tell someone that they are doing wrong and that God is unhappy with them. For example, in 2 Samuel 12, a prophet named Nathan is sent by God to tell King David that God is unhappy with him for what he did (getting a woman pregnant and having her husband killed).

You'll find in Old Testament prophecy that, although the prophets do talk about the future, just as often their prophecies (the words they're given by God) are about what's going on at the moment.

When the prophets of the Old Testament do talk about the future, a lot of times they give a kind of prophecy called *messianic* (mess-ee-ANN-ick) *prophecy*. Messianic prophecy means prophecy about the Messiah, and "Messiah" is a fancy title for Jesus. In other words, Messianic prophecy is prophecy about Jesus. The most famous example of Messianic prophecy is Isaiah 53. The Old Testament prophecy books, both major and minor, are filled with Messianic prophecy.

The first major prophet is Isaiah. He served in Judah during the reigns of four kings, two of which were evil. In his prophecies he warned that the sins of Judah and its kings would lead to captivity. However, Isaiah also spoke of redemption – what would happen to God's people after they returned to Him. A large part of the book of Isaiah deals with his prophecies about Jesus.

The next major prophet is Jeremiah, who wrote the book with his name on it and also the next book, Lamentations. Jeremiah served during the days of the last kings of Judah, and remained with those who were left behind after the captivity. Jeremiah was a sad prophet, often saying how much he cries for the people. He spoke words against the kings, against foreigners who were hostile to the Jews, and against other Jews who tried to lead the people into doing wrong.

Jeremiah's second book, Lamentations, is a very sad book. The word lamentation, or lament, means a sad poem or song, and this book is filled with sad poems. In it, Jeremiah cries loudly to God about the condition his city, Jerusalem, is in after it has been invaded by a foreign army and most of its people carried away into slavery. He talks about how a once-great city is now a ruin. And he talks about how a once-great people, the Jews, are now themselves in ruins because they've turned away from God.

The next major prophet is Ezekiel. Bible scholars have had a hard time understanding much of what Ezekiel had to say, since his book contains things that are hard to understand. However, the basic idea of Ezekiel's prophecy is that God is in charge, and that the people of Judah are in captivity because they disobeyed Him.

The last major prophet is Daniel. Daniel was a captive Jew who was also a high-ranking official in Babylon. Much of the book is the story of the things that happened to Daniel while in Babylon; he and his friends being put in a furnace for refusing to bow to the king's idol, being put in the lion's den for praying to God, etc. After a brief summary of Daniel's life, the book goes on to give Daniel's prophecies. Most of them are hard to understand, and to this day Bible scholars debate about what they mean. However, most Bible scholars agree that some of his prophecy is about Jesus, and some of it is about events in world history that haven't happened yet. It's not necessary right now to try to understand Daniel's prophecies; Bible scholars have been studying them for centuries and still don't agree about what they mean. Whatever their meaning, God is in control of it all, and our duty is to continue to worship Him and live our lives the way He wants us to.

THE MINOR PROPHETS

The twelve books of the Minor Prophets contain prophecies written at different times in history. Most were written during the time of the Divided Kingdom, a couple were written during the captivity, and two were written after the Jews returned from captivity.

Some of the prophecy of the Minor Prophets is Messianic, but most of it has to do with events going on at the time. As with the Major Prophets, the Minor Prophets warned the people that God expects His commands to be obeyed; warned other nations that the Jews were God's people; and warned the people against disobeying God and worshipping idols.

CHAPTER SEVEN

THE PERIOD BETWEEN THE TESTAMENTS

Even though the Bible is silent about what happened between the end of the Old Testament (when Nehemiah governed the people who returned from slavery and Ezra was their priest) to the beginning of the New Testament (when an angel appeared to a priest to tell him about Jesus), it's important to understand this period in history. What happened in the 400 "silent years" (as Bible scholars call them) is very important, because this period of history set the stage for Jesus' arrival in the world.

Even though the Jews had returned from slavery and re-claimed the Promised Land as their home, it was still officially a province (a country or region governed by another foreign country) of Persia (the ancient kingdom that is now the modern nation of Iran).

When they returned from captivity, the Jews were finally cured of their need to worship idols. They tore down all of the shrines and altars that their ancestors had built to idols, and they were even unkind to foreigners because they were afraid of being influenced by them to worship idols.

The Jews also developed what are called *synagogues* (SIN-uh-gawgs). A synagogue is a place where Jews could worship, and listen to sermons and lessons, apart from the Temple. Since it wasn't convenient for the Jews to go to the Temple every time they wanted to worship, they began to worship in synagogues as well as the Temple. To this day, Jews around the world worship in synagogues.

About 330 years before Jesus was born, this part of the world was conquered by a Greek (a person from Greece) named Alexander the Great. You'll read more about Alexander as you study history in school. The influence of the Greeks, under Alexander the Great, was so powerful that, by the time of Jesus, most of the educated people of the world still spoke Greek. In fact, the New Testament was written completely in Greek. Even in Jesus' day, the Jews sometimes referred to foreigners (even if they weren't Greek) as "Greeks."

Alexander the Great had also conquered Egypt, and after his death there was still a large amount of Greek influence in Egypt. After Alexander, a series of Egyptian military rulers, called Ptolemies (TALL-uh-meez) ruled the area. This was a very dark period in Jewish history. The Ptolemies were very unkind to the Jews, often killing or torturing them for minor offenses.

One of the Ptolemies, known as Antiochus (ann-TYE-uh-cuss), vandalized the Temple. He put up shrines to foreign gods, poured pig's blood on the altar (the Jews thought pigs were "unclean" and didn't touch them), and tried to force the Jews to worship idols.

In response to this, a group of people called the Maccabes (MACK-uh-beez) led a revolt against the rule of the Ptolemies, about 170 years before Jesus was born. Some of them paid for it with their lives and were tortured to death, but eventually the revolt was successful, and the Jews were once again a free nation, and remained so for about 100 years.

You may be familiar with the story of Chanukah, also known as the Festival of Lights. If you're not familiar, I'll tell the story here. It refers to the event that happened when the Jews cleaned and re-dedicated the Temple after the Ptolemies were thrown out. The Jews only had enough oil for the lamps in the Temple to burn for one night, but instead they burned for eight nights, according to tradition. Jesus and His family celebrated Chanukah, just like modern Jews today celebrate Chanukah.

About 60 years before Jesus was born, the Jews were conquered once again, this time by the Romans. You'll learn more about the Roman Empire as you study history in school. The Romans were definitely not kind to the Jews; many were tortured or killed for trying to oppose Roman rule. The Romans did allow the Jews to worship God. However, the Romans put images of their leader, Caesar (SEE-zar) in the Temple, to remind the Jews of who was in charge.

The Romans would refer to the Promised Land as *Judea* (joo-DEE-ah), after Judah, the southern half of the Divided Kingdom. Even the Jews themselves would refer to the land as either Israel or Judea.

In the 400 years between the Old Testament and the New Testament, the Jews had been free, been ruled harshly, had had another taste of freedom, and been ruled harshly again. And in that time, God had sent no prophets to comfort or warn the people (which is why Bible scholars refer to the time as the "silent years"). By the time Jesus arrived, the people were desperate for a savior.

CHAPTER EIGHT

THE GOSPELS

The word "Gospel" comes from a Greek word meaning "good news." And that is just what the Gospels are: the good news about Jesus. The four books of Matthew, Mark, Luke and John all tell the story of Jesus' life, ministry, death and resurrection. Though they tell it in different ways, and there are differences in the way they tell the various events of Jesus' life, as a whole they show us a complete picture of who Jesus was and is.

Bible scholars call the first three gospels (Matthew, Mark and Luke) the *synoptic* (sin-OPT-ick) gospels. This is a fancy way of saying that these gospels provide a synopsis (summary) of Jesus' life. The fourth gospel, John, is different. Though the first half does, in general, summarize Jesus' life and ministry, the last half of the book deals almost completely with the events of one night (the night Jesus was arrested and put on trial).

Each gospel is unique in the way it tells Jesus' story. Matthew tends to focus more on Jesus' sermons and teachings. Mark is the shortest gospel, and mostly just gives us outlines of the major events of Jesus' life; Mark also focuses on Jesus' inner spiritual life. Luke focuses on Jesus' compassion. And John, who was a close, personal friend of Jesus, tells the story of Jesus as a close companion and friend.

JESUS' FRIENDS, NEIGHBORS, AND ENEMIES

Before we get into the basics of Jesus' life and ministry, I think it's important for you to understand some of the people who lived with and dealt with Jesus in His life. This knowledge of the people of Jesus' day will give you a much better understanding of who He was and is.

1. **Priests and Levites.** You may remember from Chapter 4 of this book that God set aside people from the tribe of Levi, called Levites, to have certain jobs related to worship. Within the tribe of Levi were descendants of Aaron who were allowed to have the job of priest – another job related to worship (and a slightly more important job than that of a Levite). The most important priest of all was known as the High Priest – he was considered the final authority on all things related to Jewish worship. Many times throughout His ministry Jesus crossed paths with priests and Levites.

2. **Scribes and Teachers of the Law.** In a time in history when very few people knew how to read, scribes had the job of copying the scriptures. Since they spent their lives copying the words of the Old Testament, the scribes were very familiar with what it said, particularly with regard to the Law. Teachers of the Law were just that – people who taught the Law to the people. Usually these people were very strict and severe with regard to the Law, expecting the people to follow the Law (at least, the laws of the Sabbath and the laws of clean and unclean) to the letter, and demanding harsh punishments from those who didn't. The scribes and teachers did not take kindly to Jesus when He taught the people that He was the new Law.

3. **Pharisees and Sadducees.** Think of Pharisees (FAIR-us-eez) and Sadducees (SAD-you-seez) as college professors. They were very educated and very familiar with the Law. They also hated each other, because they both had different ideas about the Old Testament. The Pharisees, like the teachers of the Law, were very harsh, and very strict, about the people's obedience to the Law. They were also very much against the Romans being in Judea, and wanted the Romans out. The Sadducees were more interested in keeping peace with the Romans. Jesus upset the Pharisees and Sadducees with His teachings, and His behavior, quite often in the gospels.

4. **The Romans.** You may remember that I said that the Jews, after they returned from captivity, were very unkind to foreigners. Of course, it wouldn't do to be unkind to the Romans – it could cost you your life. In Jesus' day, there were several Romans about. Many were politicians, and many more were soldiers, but there were also some everyday Roman people who lived their lives in Judea. The Romans were very loyal to Caesar, their king, and for a Jew to disrespect Caesar usually carried a death sentence. Many of the Romans could be cruel, but in general, if you were a Jew the Romans left you alone if you paid your taxes, did as you were told, minded your own business and didn't try to start trouble.

5. **Tax Collectors.** One thing the Romans were good at was collecting taxes. The job of tax collector was one that the Romans usually gave to certain Jews to handle. The Jews hated the tax collectors. For one thing, they felt that the tax collectors were traitors to their people for making them pay money to Rome. For another thing, many tax collectors weren't honest and took more than they were supposed to, keeping the extra for themselves. Jesus was kind to the tax collectors; in fact, the gospel of Matthew was written by a tax collector, Matthew, who became one of Jesus' disciples.

6. **Sinners.** The Jewish leaders had very little kindness for people who committed sin, often demanding harsh punishment and generally treating them cruelly. Jesus, however, had kindness and compassion for people who sinned, telling them that He forgave them and asking them to follow Him.

7. **Samaritans.** You may remember that, during the captivity, a few people were left behind. These were generally the poorest, least educated, and sometimes disabled. Those who were left behind were forced to marry foreigners and have children with them. The descendants of these people were called Samaritans (suh-MARE-it-uhns), after Samaria, the city that had been the capital of the northern kingdom of Israel during the time of the divided kingdom. The Jews were very unkind to the Samaritans – they believed that they were traitors to the Jewish people and religion because they had foreign blood in them. The Jews would not help the Samaritans or even talk to them. In fact, when a Jew needed to go from one end of Judea to the other, rather than walk through Samaria, they walked around it, going several dozen miles out of their way, simply to avoid contact with a Samaritan.

8. **The Disciples.** The word *disciple* (diss-SYE-puhl) means "student" or "follower." Another word for disciple is *apostle* (uh-POSS-uhl), which means the same thing. Jesus selected 12 men to be His assistants and friends, who would carry on His ministry after He died. These men are referred to as the Twelve Disciples, the Twelve Apostles, or just The Twelve, throughout the New Testament.

JESUS' BIRTH AND EARLY LIFE

Now that we understand the type of people that Jesus lived with and ministered to, we can begin the story of Jesus. Matthew begins by giving us what is known as a *genealogy* (jee-nee-AL-uh-jee), a list of ancestors, of Jesus. Luke does the same thing, but in a different way.

Matthew tells us that an angel visited Joseph, Jesus' father, to tell him that the Savior was going to be born. Luke starts a little earlier in the story, first telling us about the events that led up to the birth of John the Baptist (who will be important later in the story). Then Luke tells us about an angel visiting Mary, Jesus' mother, to tell her the good news that she would be the mother of the Savior.

Luke's story of Jesus' birth is the story we are most familiar with, and what we celebrate at Christmas. Luke tells us of Mary & Joseph's journey to Bethlehem (so they could register to pay Roman taxes), how Jesus was born in a stable because there was no room at the inn, and how angels appeared to shepherds to tell the good news of the Savior being born.

Very little is known about Jesus' childhood. We know from Matthew 2:1-12 that wise men from the east visited Jesus and gave Him gifts, and that Jesus and His family spent some time in Egypt (Matthew 2:13-23), and at age 12 Jesus went with his family to the Temple and amazed the older, educated teachers there (Luke 2:41-52). Other than that, we know next to nothing about Jesus' life before His ministry began.

This is where John the Baptist, who I told you about earlier in this chapter, comes in. Luke tells us that John's mother, Elizabeth, and Jesus' mother, Mary, visited each other before either boy was born (Luke 1:39-45). About thirty years later, John had a ministry baptizing people in the Jordan river. Baptism is a ceremony where someone is dunked under water to demonstrate their willingness to repent from their sin. Even though Jesus had no sin, He still allowed John to baptize Him (Matthew 3:15).

After His baptism, Jesus went into the desert to fast (go without food) and pray for 40 days. During this time, the devil tried to tempt Him (Luke 4:1-13), but Jesus didn't give in to temptation. He was now ready to start His ministry.

JESUS' MINISTRY

Several books have been written about Jesus' ministry; so many that they could fill several dozen whole libraries. The gospels tell us the story of Jesus' ministry, and they each tell of different events (though some events are repeated, but told in a slightly different way, in different gospels), and they tell them in different orders. For these reasons, the best thing I can do, as your author, is to give you a general outline of the basics of Jesus' ministry.

1. **Jesus taught in sermons.** A sermon is a long discussion of a topic, like what your minister does every Sunday in church. Several of Jesus' sermons are recorded in the gospels. Jesus' most famous sermon is known as the Sermon on the Mount (the Mount is the Mount of Olives, a hill near Jerusalem). You can read the Sermon on the Mount in Matthew 5-7.

   One of the most important themes in all of Jesus' sermons is this: a religion based on strict lists of do's and don'ts, and harsh punishments for doing wrong, is not what God wants for His people. God's law should be based on love, and God's people should honor God through love, not through obeying lists of rules. Jesus said, in Matthew 7:12, that all of the Law and all of the Prophets (that is, all of the instructions in the Law and the words of all of the prophets, major and minor) can be summed up in this: love God with everything you have, and treat other people the way you want to be treated.

2. **Jesus taught in parables.** A parable is a story that teaches a point. Usually in parables, people and objects are used to represent certain concepts or ideas. For example, you may be familiar with the parable of the Good Samaritan. Jesus uses this parable to teach that we need to love people even if we don't think they're good enough (you'll remember that the Jews were very unkind to the Samaritans).

3. **Jesus healed people.** All throughout the gospels are stories of Jesus using His power to heal people. He healed people no matter who they were, or what religion the followed.

4. **Jesus performed miracles.** Several times in Jesus' ministry, He used miracles to show that He was really God's son. Here are just a few examples: At a wedding, He turned water into wine. When some friends of His were sad that another friend (Lazarus) had died, He raised Lazarus from the dead. He fed 5,000 people with five loaves of bread and two fishes (all four gospels tell us about this miracle).

5. **Jesus befriended (made friends with) people that the Jews hated.** Jesus didn't heal people, befriend people, or select people to be His disciples based on their wealth, their ancestry, or their social position. He only cared about the peoples' faith in Him. He healed a Roman soldier's daughter, even though the Jews hated the Romans (and other foreigners). One of His disciples was a tax collector, even though the Jews hated tax collectors. He ministered in Samaria and made friends with Samaritans, even though the Jews hated Samaritans. One of his closest friends was a woman who had led an immoral life. Jesus told all of these people to stop sinning and follow Him, and they did.

6. **Jesus chose disciples.** The word "disciple" here just means "follower," and in His ministry Jesus had thousands of followers. However, He also chose twelve men to be His closest friends, who would help Him in His ministry and would carry on His ministry after He died. It's not important right now to know the names of all twelve, but remember these names: Matthew (who wrote a gospel and was a tax collector), John (who wrote a gospel, was probably Jesus' closest friend, and wrote several other New Testament books), and Peter (who wrote two New Testament books and is a very important person in the early history of Christianity).

7. **Jesus taught what was really important in people.** The Jews of Jesus' time believed that wealth, respect, and power were the most important things a person could have. They taught that, if a person had those things, it was because they obeyed the Law, and if someone was poor or disabled, it was because they had sin in their life. Their religion was one of making a good appearance on the outside; but Jesus taught that what really matters is what is in your heart. To teach this, He told a parable about a poor woman making an offering in the Temple. He said that a rich man, dressed in fancy clothes, made sure everyone was watching him as he put his generous offering of money in the Temple collection box, while next to him a very poor woman put two worthless coins in the box. Jesus taught that the poor woman's offering was worth more to God than the rich man's, because the woman gave from her heart, while the man was just doing it to be seen and admired.

8. **Jesus upset the religious leaders.** The high-ranking Jewish leaders would often get upset with Jesus because He did things that they thought violated the Law. When Jesus spat on the ground to make clay so He could put it on a blind man's eyes and heal the man's blindness, the leaders got upset with him for spitting on the Sabbath. They didn't care at all that a blind man had been healed; they were concerned with someone breaking their idea of Sabbath law! Jesus called the leaders hypocrites (people who say one thing and do another) because they were concerned with making a good appearance, but their hearts were evil. They even got upset with Jesus because He didn't wash His hands before He ate! Mostly, though, they were upset with Jesus because He was a challenge to their way of life. Jesus taught that God is a God of love, not a God of lists of rules. The leaders, however, believed that Law was all there was. They drew their power from the Law. The Law made them different from the Romans and the foreigners that they hated. The Law was what

made them Jews, and without it, they had nothing (at least, that's what they believed).

THE END OF JESUS' LIFE

Jesus' ministry lasted about three years, and by the end of it the Jewish leaders were quite sick of Him. The people were beginning to follow Jesus, and the Jewish leaders feared that the people would turn to Him and away from them (there's more to the story, but this is enough for you to understand, for now).

One of Jesus' disciples, named Judas, made a deal with the priests. For thirty pieces of silver, he would betray Jesus when an angry mob came to arrest him. After He was arrested, Jesus was brought to the chief priest's house to be put on trial. The Jewish leaders took a vote and decided that Jesus was guilty of blasphemy (speaking against God) and should be put to death.

The Jews wanted Jesus dead, but according to Roman law they couldn't execute anyone without Rome's permission. The Romans, though they were sometimes cruel, were at least fair enough to not put anybody to death without a trial. The Jewish leaders first brought Him to Pilate (a Roman official). Pilate didn't think Jesus was doing anything wrong, so he sent Him to Herod (a higher-ranking official). Herod didn't thing Jesus was doing anything wrong, either, so he sent Him back to Pilate.

Pilate had two prisoners in his prison: Jesus and a murderer named Barabbas (bur-RABB-uss). Pilate had a tradition that he would release a prisoner, free and clear, every Passover (Passover was coming up). The people asked for Barabbas, and even though Pilate wanted to let Jesus go free, he let Barabbas go. So why didn't he let Jesus go, too? Because he was afraid that the people would start a riot, and the Romans would usually do whatever they could to avoid a riot. (Again, there's a lot more to the story, but this is enough for you to understand, for now.)

Jesus was ordered to be crucified – the most humiliating and painful death the Romans could have imagined. Crucifixion involves nailing the victim to a cross through their wrists and ankles, dropping the cross in a deep hole so the victim's shoulders dislocate, and allowing the victim to suffer for several hours until he dies of suffocation. The Bible teaches us that Jesus was on the cross for about six hours before He died.

THE RESURRECTION

Luke tells us that a wealthy man name Joseph asked for Jesus' body to be placed in a tomb (grave) that he owned. Jesus' body was dressed in burial clothes and prepared with spices, following the customs of the time. The tomb was then sealed with a huge stone, and two Roman guards were sent to guard the tomb.

The gospels tell us different versions of what happened next, but the basic story is this: two women who were friends of Jesus went to the tomb and found it empty and the guards gone. They were both sad and frightened, but Jesus appeared to them to comfort them. Jesus later appeared to His disciples and announced that He had come back from the dead. They were frightened, and didn't want to believe it, but eventually they believed.

Matthew tells us that Jesus, before He left for the final time, gave the disciples instructions. Those instructions appear in Matthew 28:18-20, and Bible scholars call these instructions The Great Commission. In it, Jesus tells the disciples to go throughout the whole world and to spread the good news about Him, and to make believers out of the whole world. This Commission would guide the disciples in what they did as they spread throughout the known world, telling the good news of Jesus, and laying the foundation for the Christian church. This story is told in the next section of the New Testament: the book of Acts.

CHAPTER NINE

NEW TESTAMENT HISTORY: ACTS

In the Old Testament, the books of history contain twelve books; many of them are extremely long and contain long lists of names and places. The New Testament, on the other hand, only has one book of history: the book of Acts. This is the story of what Jesus' disciples did after Jesus left, and how they started the Christian church.

The book was written by Luke, who also wrote a gospel. In the first paragraph of the book, we see that the book was written for one man, whom Luke calls Theophilus (thee-AHF-uh-luss). You may remember that I said that Luke's gospel focused on Jesus' compassion. In the gospel of Luke, Luke pays special attention to people that were normally treated poorly in Jesus' day: the poor; women; Samaritans; foreigners; and people like that. The book of Acts is much the same way. Also, since Theophilus wasn't a Jew (he may have been a Roman), Luke spends a lot of time, both in his gospel and in Acts, explaining Jewish customs.

In this chapter, I'll talk about Luke quite a bit. When you read the words "Luke tells us..." in this chapter, I'm talking about Luke as the author of this book, Acts. I'm not talking about Luke's gospel. Also, keep in mind that Luke himself was involved in some of the events that happened in the book of Acts.

The story begins with Jesus on earth after His resurrection. Jesus spent forty days on earth after the resurrection, teaching the disciples, and telling them that something big was about to happen. Acts 1:5 says: "For John [the Baptist] baptized with water, but in a few days you will be baptized with the Holy Spirit." We'll find out what this means in a little bit.

Jesus then *ascended* into Heaven. The word "ascended" means that Jesus floated up into the sky until the disciples couldn't see Him any more. Luke tells us that, as they were looking into the sky, two angels appeared to them and told them that Jesus would one day return to earth the same way He went to Heaven (Acts 1:11).

The disciples next had to find someone to replace Judas. You'll remember that Jesus' disciple Judas had betrayed Jesus. Out of guilt for what he did, Judas took his own life. That left eleven disciples, and they needed twelve, so they chose a man named Matthias (muh-THY-us) (Acts 1:26).

The second chapter of the book of Acts is very important, both in Christian history, and in the lives of Christians today. Luke tells us that the disciples were in a room celebrating the feast of Pentecost (PENT-uh-cost), a Jewish holiday. The disciples heard a sound that sounded like a strong wind, and then something that looked like tongues made of fire fell on them (Acts 2:3)

This was the gift of the Holy Spirit that Jesus had promised in chapter 1. The Holy Spirit is a gift from God that works in the life of a Christian. If you are a Christian and you have been baptized, you have the gift of the Holy Spirit. Several books have been written about the Holy Spirit, and it would take several pages for me to try to explain this gift, but that is not the focus of this book. If you are interested in learning more about the Holy Spirit, I encourage you to talk to your parents or a youth leader.

In the book of Acts, the Holy Spirit gave the disciples special abilities. First, they were able to "speak in tongues" – in other words, the disciples were able to speak in foreign languages that they had never studied. This was helpful to the disciples at this time in history: when they went to foreign countries to share the good news about Jesus, they were able to speak the language! They were also given the ability to heal people; several times in the book of Acts Luke tells us about the disciples healing people. They were also given other special abilities by the Holy Spirit, but the gifts of tongues (speaking foreign languages) and healing are the most important to know about for now.

Some Christians today believe that the Holy Spirit still gives Christians the power to speak in tongues or to heal (or both). They even make speaking in tongues a part of their worship. Other Christians believe that the gift of tongues was a one-time only gift to the Christians of the first century (the time when the events in the book of Acts take place). This is a debate for Bible scholars and is not the focus of this book.

With the gift of the Holy Spirit, the disciples now had the power to go out and spread the good news about Jesus. They began their ministry in Jerusalem. In fact, Luke tells us in Acts 2 and 3 about things that Peter and

John did in Jerusalem, and even tells us what Peter preached in his sermons in Jerusalem.

Acts 4 and 5 tell us about some other events in the early church – in particular, how the early Christians shared their money and their belongings and lived with one another.

Now would be a good time to talk about what is meant by the word "church" as it appears in the New Testament. You may think of a church as a building, with walls, floors, windows, etc, where people come together to worship on Sunday morning. That's a good definition of what a church is, but in the New Testament, the word "church" meant something more.

The Greek word (remember, the New Testament was written in Greek) that we translate as "church" can also mean "community." A community is more than just a village or city or neighborhood or point on a map. A community is a group of people who all have the same purpose. In the book of Acts, that community was the first Christians – the group of people whose purpose was to serve Jesus and live according to His teachings.

The book of Acts tells us that the early Christians truly lived as a community. They looked out for each other, prayed for each other, cared for each other, and met one another's needs. They even took it a step further – they sold their belongings and shared money with one another.

Today, most Christian groups don't generally live together and share their money with one another, but the example of the early church is still a good one. A church should be more than just a building where people gather on Sunday morning, worship for a while, then leave. A church should be a community of Christians who have friendships with one another, who pray for each other and care for each other.

Just like Jesus had angered the Jewish leaders of the day, the disciples began to anger the Jewish leaders as well. They were not happy that the disciples were preaching that Jesus had risen from the dead – in fact, they weren't happy that the disciples were mentioning Jesus at all. Several times throughout the book of Acts Luke tells us about the disciples being tortured or put in jail because of their ministry.

When one group of people harasses or tries to do harm to another group of people, it's called *persecution* (per-suh-KYU-shun), and this is what was happening to the disciples, they were being persecuted by the Jewish leaders. In Acts 6 & 7 we learn about a man named Stephen, who was a Christian who was put in charge of distributing food to the poor (Acts 6:1-5). Some Jewish leaders got upset with Stephen and convinced a crowd to riot against him. In Acts 7, we learn about Stephen's death at the hand of a crowd of rioters. Bible scholars say that Stephen was the first Christian *martyr* (MAR-ter); a martyr is someone who dies for what they believe in.

With Stephen's death, two things happened: 1) a persecution against Christians broke out in and around Jerusalem (at the time, this meant that anyone who claimed to be a Christian would probably risk being killed); and 2) the disciples began preaching in Samaria.

You'll remember from the previous chapter that the Jews hated the Samaritans, and that Jesus treated the Samaritans with kindness. Following Jesus' example, His disciples went to Samaria to preach the good news. We also read about a high-ranking foreign official becoming a Christian – this is important, because this shows that Christianity was becoming a religion for everybody, not just Jews.

One of the most important people in the New Testament enters the picture at this time. A man named Saul was one of the Jews who was persecuting the Christians. In fact, Saul was so eager to kill Christians that he got the permission of the high priest to go to Damascus (a foreign city) to find Christians there and bring them to Jerusalem to be put in prison.

On the way to Damascus (duh-MASS-cus), Jesus appeared to Saul. Jesus told Saul that he (Saul) was persecuting Him (Jesus). Jesus then made Saul blind and told him go to Damascus and wait for instructions. In Damascus, Jesus told a man named Ananias (ann-nuh-NYE-us) to go to Saul and lay his hands on him (laying hands on someone was a way of appointing them to an important job). Ananias did what Jesus asked him to do; he prayed for Saul and laid his hands on him. Saul's eyesight then came back to him.

Saul would eventually change his name to Paul, and he would become the main person in the second half of the book of Acts. Many Bible scholars believe that Jesus Himself chose Saul to be His messenger to the world outside of Israel. Saul had three things going for him. First, he spoke Greek. This made him able to preach the good news in foreign countries (since Greek was spoken all throughout the ancient world), and made him acceptable to the educated people of the day (the people of the day considered it a sign of good education if you spoke Greek). Second, Paul was a Roman citizen. Being a Roman citizen gave you special rights and privileges that ordinary people didn't have, especially when it came to dealing with the Roman government. And third, Paul was a Pharisee (remember what I said about Pharisees from the previous chapter); this made him a knowledgeable person who could hold his own in debate and conversation with the educated Jews.

But before we turn our attention to Paul, we must go back to Peter. You'll remember that, earlier in this book, I said that very few foreigners converted to Judaism. In Acts 10, we meet a foreigner, a Roman official named Cornelius, who worshipped God and served Him. An angel told Cornelius to have Peter come and meet with him.

Peter was, and had always been, a devout Jew. You'll remember that Jews were not always kind to foreigners, especially Romans. Even after spending time with Jesus and watching as Jesus made friends with and ministered to foreigners, Peter's old Jewish attitudes still affected his outlook on life. God had to get through to Peter, so God sent Peter a vision. It's not necessary to go into the details of the vision right now, but here's the important part of the vision: God made it clear to Peter that the good news about Jesus was for everybody; not just Jews, but also Gentiles (JEN-tiles).

"Gentile" is a word that is used in the New Testament to describe someone who is not a Jew. In general, this is how Jews would politely refer to foreigners or non-Jews. In this book, I've used the word "foreigner" to describe people who weren't Jews, but for the rest of the book I'll use the term Gentile, since it's the term the Bible uses.

The fact that God told Peter to preach the good news about Jesus to the Gentiles marks a turning point in Christian history. Until that time, the worship of God had been the religion of a small ethnic group that mostly lived on the eastern shores of the Mediterranean Sea. Now, God was making it clear that He wanted all the people of the world, regardless of their race or ethnic group, to worship Him.

This was probably a little hard for Peter and the other early Christian leaders to take. They had been Jews all their lives, and Jews were generally unkind to Gentiles. Often, the early Christians would get in more trouble for preaching to the Gentiles than they would for preaching about Jesus in the first place. In fact, the relationship between Jewish Christians and Gentile Christians would become a major source of problems later on.

Beginning in chapter 13, Paul begins to become the main focus of the book of Acts. It's not necessary at this time to get into detail about everything that Paul did, but there are a few points that you should know. Basically, Paul became the missionary (you'll remember that a missionary is someone who goes to a foreign country to teach about Jesus) to the Gentiles. He took the good news of Jesus Christ and preached it in the major cities throughout the ancient Roman world. Some of these cities still stand to this day (Rome, Athens), and others are now ruins (Corinth, Ephesus). By preaching in these major cities, he was able to spread Christianity from the area around Jerusalem to the whole world. If you are a Christian, you have Paul to thank. Because of Paul's preaching to the ancient cities of what is now Europe (especially Rome), Europe became Christian. When European settlers came to what is now the United States of America, they were Christians. If you are a descendant of those settlers, you are a Christian because of Paul's preaching.

You will hear your minister or Sunday school teacher talk about Paul's Missionary Journeys. Paul took three journeys in his life, going to different places throughout the Roman world and preaching the good news. Sometimes he was put in prison or tortured; sometimes he healed or performed other miracles; at one point he barely survived a shipwreck (more on this in a few pages); but mostly, he preached. Everywhere he went, he told everyone who would listen all about the good news of Jesus.

In addition to Paul and his journeys, there are two major themes that are important in the second half of the book of Acts, and they are closely related to each other.

The first theme is the relationship between Jewish Christians and Gentile Christians. In Acts 7, we read that Gentile widows were being overlooked in favor of Jewish widows as food was being distributed to the poor each day. In Acts 15 we learn that some of the Jewish Christians were teaching that, in order to become a Christian, one had to be a Jew first. In other words, a Gentile who converted to Christianity must first go through the Jewish ritual of circumcision. The original disciples, and Paul, made it clear that circumcision was not necessary. To be a Christian one didn't have to be a Jew first. Paul also made it clear that Gentile Christians and Jewish Christians were all just Christians, and they needed to not treat each other differently because of their nationality. Despite the teachings of Paul, Peter, and the early Christian leaders on this subject, the relationship between Jewish Christians and Gentile Christians would be a problem in the early Christian church for several years.

The second theme is the beginning of Christianity as a separate religion. At first, the Jews, the people who practiced other religions, and even the Christians themselves believed that Christianity was a sect (a sect is a small group) within Judaism. However, with Gentiles being converted to Christianity, and skipping Judaism in the process, it became clear that Christianity was, and is, a separate religion entirely. Acts 11:26 tells us that, in the ancient city of Antioch, people first started using the word "Christian."

The book of Acts concludes with Paul's journey to Rome. On his missionary journeys, Paul hadn't been to Rome. In a lot of ways, however, Rome was Paul's final and most important destination. Rome was the center of the Roman Empire, and was the most powerful city in the world at the time. By getting to Rome, Paul would be able to bring the good news about Jesus to the most influential city in the world.

Paul was in Jerusalem preaching when the Jewish leaders tried to have him imprisoned. The crowd almost rioted, and the Romans got involved (remember, the Romans were very cautious when it came to riots). Paul was sent from one Roman official to the next. Each one found him innocent but didn't know what to do with him. Paul got sick of it and asked for a trial before Caesar, the Roman king. As a Roman citizen, Paul had the right to ask for a trial before Caesar.

It was on the journey to Rome for his trial before Caesar that Paul was shipwrecked, on an island in the Mediterranean Sea called Malta (Acts 27:27 - 28:10). While there, Paul preached the good news about Jesus to the Romans there and to the local Maltans.

The book of Acts concludes with Paul's arrival in Rome. He was placed under house arrest (which meant that he could not leave his home), but he continued to preach to the Romans. The book doesn't tell us what happened to Paul after his arrival in Rome, but we know from history that he was eventually beheaded.

In addition to his missionary journeys, Paul spent a lot of time writing letters to churches that he had started, and to other Christians. Paul wrote some of them from prison, and wrote others when he was free. Those letters appear in the next section of the New Testament.

CHAPTER TEN

THE PAULINE AND GENERAL EPISTLES

Bible scholars refer to the next thirteen books of the New Testament (the thirteen that come after to book of Acts) as the *Pauline Epistles* (PAUL-een uh-PIS-uhls). "Pauline" is just a fancy way of saying "written by Paul," and "epistle" is just a fancy word for "letter." So in other words, "Pauline Epistles" means "letters written by Paul."

The next eight books of the New Testament are called the *General Epistles.* This means that they are general letters; that is, letters not written by Paul.

The titles of the Pauline Epistles (Romans, 1 Corinthians, etc.) refer to the people that Paul intended to read his letters. For example, Paul's letter entitled Romans was meant to be read by the church in Rome. 1 Corinthians was the first of two letters we have that Paul wrote to the church in the ancient city of Corinth, and 2 Corinthians is the second. The General Epistles are known by the name of their writer. Here is a list of the names of the letters in the New Testament, who wrote them, and who the intended readers were. *Note: In this table, if a city is in ruins or no longer exists, I refer to it as "the ancient city of _____."

Romans	Paul	The Christian church in the city of Rome
1 Corinthians	Paul	The Christian church in the ancient city of Corinth (this is the first of two such letters)

2 Corinthians	Paul	The Christian church in the ancient city of Corinth (this is the second of two such letters)
Galatians	Paul	The Christian church in the region of the ancient world known as Galatia
Ephesians	Paul	The Christian church in the ancient city of Ephesus
Philippians	Paul	The Christian church in the ancient city of Phillippi
Colossians	Paul	The Christian church in the ancient city of Colosse
1 Thessalonians	Paul	The Christian church in the city of Thessalonica (this is the first of two such letters)
2 Thessalonians	Paul	The Christian church in the city of Thessalonica (this is the second of two such letters)
1 Timothy	Paul	A friend of Paul's named Timothy, who was involved in ministry in the church (this is the first of two such letters) *See first note.
2 Timothy	Paul	A friend of Paul's named Timothy, who was involved in ministry in the church (this is the second of two such letters) * See first note.
Titus	Paul	A friend of Paul's named Titus, who was involved in ministry in the church
Philemon	Paul	A friend of Paul's named Philemon, who owned a slave that had run away and stayed with Paul
Hebrews	Unknown*	To Jewish Christians throughout the ancient world * See second note
James	James*	To Jewish Christians throughout the ancient world *See third note

1 Peter	Peter	To Christians throughout the ancient world (this is the first of two such letters) *See fourth note
2 Peter	Peter	To Christians throughout the ancient world (this is the second of two such letters)
1 John	John*	To Christians throughout the ancient world (this is the first of three such letters) *See fifth note
2 John	John	To a personal friend of John whom he calls the "chosen lady and her children"
3 John	John	To a personal friend of John's name Gaius
Jude	Jude	To Christians throughout the ancient world *See sixth note

Notes

1. Bible scholars refer to the letters to Timothy and Titus as the *Pastoral* (pass-TORE-ole) *Epistles*. This is because Paul was acting as a pastor (a person who leads and cares for another person or a group) to Timothy and Titus, and also because Timothy and Titus were both pastors of churches.
2. Bible scholars are not sure who wrote Hebrews (since the author did not identify himself in the letter, as they do in the other letters). To this day, Bible scholars debate about whether Paul wrote Hebrews or another writer wrote it. Most Bible scholars believe that Paul did not write it, so in this book it's considered a General Epistle.
3. The James who wrote this book was probably Jesus' brother (Bible scholars debate about this).
4. Peter was one of Jesus' disciples.
5. John was one of Jesus' disciples, the same John who wrote the gospel of John.
6. Jude calls himself the brother of James. If he was the brother of the James who was the brother of Jesus, then this means that Jude was also a brother of Jesus.

Rather than go through each of the epistles book by book, it would be easier for me to give you a general idea of what kinds of things the epistles say, as a whole. Here is a list of some of the kinds of things you'll find as you study the epistles.

1. **Instructions on How Christians Should Treat Each Other.** The Jewish Christian/Gentile Christian problem comes up often in the epistles, and the writers (Paul especially) try to remind Christians that, in Christ, we are all the same; and that it is NOT necessary to first become a Jew in order to become a Christian. There are also instructions for how husbands and wives should treat each other, how children and parents should treat each other, how wealthy Christians should treat poor Christians, etc.

2. **Instructions on How the Church Should be Managed.** The letters in the New Testament contain advice for the church as to how problems in the church should be dealt with; how leaders should be given their jobs; how worship should be conducted; etc.

3. **Doctrine.** "Doctrine" is a fancy word that Bible Scholars like to use. It simply means "facts about the Christian faith." As you study the Bible throughout your life, you'll learn quite a bit of doctrine. For now, don't worry about how much you know and don't know; a lifetime of Bible study isn't enough to learn everything there is to know about the Christian faith!

4. **Instructions on How Christians Should Live Their Lives.** The New Testament gives Christians some guidelines on how they should live their day-to-day lives; these are things you'll learn as you study the Bible throughout your life.

5. **Encouragement.** The Christians who read the letters were often being persecuted; sometimes, the writers themselves were being persecuted (in fact, Paul wrote many of his letters from a prison cell). Many of the passages in the epistles were meant to give encouragement to Christians who were being persecuted. Often, the writer asked for prayers because he was being persecuted.

6. **Prophecy.** There are a very few passages in the epistles where the writer talks about future events.

7. **Specific Instructions to Specific Readers.** There are a few passages in the epistles where one specific person is given specific instructions; for example, in 2 Timothy 4:13, Paul gives instructions to Timothy about what clothes he should pack for a journey! Obviously, such instructions are not for Christians today to obey.

The epistles are an important part of the Bible; in fact, most of the Christian churches throughout the world are, in one way or another, managed according to the instructions found in the epistles. Ministers throughout the world conduct their ministries based on the advice Paul gave to Timothy and Titus. The doctrines found in the epistles (together with those taught in the gospels) and instructions for the Christian life found in the epistles (together with those found in the gospels) are the basis for the entire Christian faith. And persecuted Christians the world over find encouragement in the words given to persecuted Christians who lived and died centuries before them.

CHAPTER ELEVEN

NEW TESTAMENT PROPHECY: REVELATION

You may, from time to time, hear a minister on TV try to scare you by quoting a passage from Revelation. Or, you may watch a movie where a character quotes Revelation in order to scare another character. After all, the book of Revelation is a book of prophecy about the end of the world; at least, that's what a lot of people believe.

While it's true that the book of Revelation contains a lot of scary passages that seem to talk about the end of the world, and that are hard to understand, there's a lot more to the story.

John, Jesus' disciple (who also wrote the gospel of John and three epistles), wrote the book of Revelation (and please remember that it's Revelation and not Revelation**s** – there is no s at the end). Most Bible scholars believe that the book was written around 90 A.D. (about sixty years after Jesus died), when John was around 80-90 years old. John was living in exile (that means that he had been forced to leave his country) on an island in the Mediterranean Sea called Patmos.

You'll remember from the chapter about Old Testament prophecy that, although prophets sometimes talk about future events, a far more important job of a prophet is to talk about what is going on at the moment. Revelation begins with prophecy about things that were going on at the moment.

The first three chapters of the book of Revelation deal with Jesus appearing to John and John describing what he sees about how Jesus appears. Then, Jesus gives words of advice and instruction to what Bible scholars call the Seven Churches of Asia Minor. When you think of Asia, you may think of the large continent that includes the countries of China, Japan, Korea, etc. But in the New Testament, the word Asia refers to a much smaller place: basically the area that is the modern nation of Turkey. There were seven Christian communities in that region, and Jesus had words to say to each of them.

After the prophecies to the seven churches of Asia Minor, the book of Revelation moves into a series of visions that John sees and describes. This is where things start to get a little tricky.

Remember, prophecy is as much about what is going on right now as much as it is about future events. Keep this in mind when we talk about what God tells us in the rest of the book of Revelation.

Two major things had happened in world history by the time John wrote the book. First, around 64 A.D. the Roman emperor Nero had started a worldwide persecution against Christians. Nero had ordered Rome to be burned down so he could re-build Rome and name it after him; about a fourth of the city burned, and several Romans lost their lives and homes. Nero didn't want the people to know that he was behind it, so he blamed the Christians, and the Romans bought his lie. For this reason, not only was the Roman government against the Christians, but so were the Roman citizens themselves. During this time, Christians were regularly tortured to death in gruesome and horrifying ways.

Second, in A.D. 70 Jerusalem was completely and thoroughly destroyed by the Romans. Historians point to this date as the end of the Jewish state. After this date, the Jews scattered throughout the world. The Promised Land became a wasteland that was occupied by nomadic ("nomadic" means "wandering") tribes for several centuries. In fact, it wasn't until the 1960's that Israel became a nation again.

With this in mind (the destruction of Jerusalem by Rome and the worldwide persecution of Christians by Rome), you can understand that God was not at all pleased with the Roman Empire. So John's visions that follow in the book of Revelation are, for the most part, prophecies that deal with the Roman Empire.

John describes these visions in language that is difficult to understand and is, in fact, kind of scary sometimes (for example, the book talks about dragons coming up out of the sea). Bible scholars describe some of these visions as *apocalyptic* (uh-pock-uh-LIP-tick) visions. The word "apocalyptic" is a fancy way of saying "referring to the end of the world."

So these prophecies in the book of Revelation are about the end of the world, right? Well, yes and no. You'll remember that I said earlier that God was very angry with Rome at this time in history. Bible scholars agree that much of what John describes in the book of Revelation has to do with things that eventually happened to Roman emperors and to the Roman Empire as a whole. Much of what remains is apocalyptic prophecy that hasn't happened yet.

The problem is that, because the language of the book of Revelation is so difficult to understand, Bible scholars don't agree with each other about what prophecies have already been fulfilled (that is, they've already happened), and what prophecies haven't yet been fulfilled. There's no doubt that some of the prophecies of Revelation were fulfilled by events in ancient Rome, and that some of them still have yet to happen. But the dividing line between what applied to Rome and what still applies to Christians today isn't clear, and Bible scholars don't agree with each other about the meaning of it all.

So what does this mean for the Christian today? Throughout the gospels, Jesus makes three things very clear about His return (which will be the start of the end of the world). First, Jesus makes it clear that no one knows when His return will be except God. Second, Jesus says that His return will take place in an instant and without warning; it may happen a million years after you've died, it may happen before you finish reading this paragraph. Third, and most importantly, trying to figure out when Jesus is returning is a pointless way to spend your time.

In other words, the end of the world prophecies in Revelation (and also Daniel, Ezekiel, and a few other places in both Testaments) are clues that only God knows the true meaning of. To spend your time worrying about what the clues mean or about when and how the world is going to end is not how God wants you to spend your time. If you see a preacher or a teacher on TV telling you that this world event or that world event was prophesied about in the book of Revelation, he is probably trying to scare you so you'll buy his books. Jesus will return when God has decided that Jesus will return. It may be in your lifetime, and it may not. Your job as a Christian is to focus on honoring God with your life, and on telling your friends about Jesus.

And this, friends, is where this book ends. If you've read this book from beginning to end, you now know more about the Bible than I did when I enrolled in Bible college. There is a lot that I left out, but the things that I left out are things that you will learn as you grow in your faith, if you make the commitment to learning them.

Your church will be your lifeline to becoming not only a more knowledgeable Christian, but also a better Christian in general. Knowing facts about the Bible is one thing; living a Christian life is another thing. Your church will help you with both. Make the commitment now to do all you can, not only as a kid but as a teenager and as an adult, to learn more about the Bible and to learn more about the Christian life. With your parents' permission, go to church and Sunday school every Sunday – and if your church offers children's church, go to that too (if you're not too old). If your church offers a mid-week children or youth gathering, go to that. Whenever there is a trip, barbecue, get-together, or any event for kids at your church, go to that. Go to every VBS (Vacation Bible School), camp, and every other event that your church offers.

As I said at the beginning of this book, this book doesn't even begin to cover everything there is to know about the Bible, or about God, or about the Christian life. No book ever will cover everything. But, I hope that it has been a starting point for you on your journey toward becoming a Christian who is knowledgeable about his or her faith.